Cakes

Cakes

for the ultimate sweet sensation

This edition published by Parragon Books Ltd in 2013
LOVE FOOD is an imprint of Parragon Books Ltd

Parragon Books Ltd
Chartist House
15–17 Trim Street
Bath BA1 1HA, UK
www.parragon.com/lovefood

ISBN 978-1-4723-0424-7

Printed in China

Notes for the Reader
This book uses both metric and imperial measurements. Follow the same units of
measurement throughout; do not mix metric and imperial. All spoon measurements are
level: teaspoons are assumed to be 5 ml, and tablespoons are assumed to be 15 ml. Unless
otherwise stated, milk is assumed to be full fat, eggs and individual vegetables are medium,
and pepper is freshly ground black pepper.

Garnishes, decorations and serving suggestions are all optional and not necessarily
included in the recipe ingredients or method. The times given are an approximate guide only.
Preparation times differ according to the techniques used by different people and the cooking
times may also vary from those given. Optional ingredients, variations or serving suggestions
have not been included in the time calculations.

Recipes using raw or very lightly cooked eggs should be avoided by infants, the elderly,
pregnant women, convalescents and anyone suffering from an illness. Pregnant and
breastfeeding women are advised to avoid eating peanuts and peanut products. Sufferers
from nut allergies should be aware that some of the ready-made ingredients used in the
recipes in this book may contain nuts. Always check the packaging before use.

Contents

Introduction

Nothing can beat the sight and taste of a freshly baked cake. Even if you're not a domestic god or goddess, the good news is that home-made cakes don't have to be difficult or time-consuming. This book is packed with delicious cakes for all occasions, so you'll never be short of ideas for easy, irresistible home-baked treats.

Few types of cooking offer more rewards than home-baking. Not only can you make superb cakes for your family and friends, but the actual hands-on process of baking is immensely satisfying and you'll be surprised by how much fun it can be.

The basic skills of cake-making are really easy to learn and you need very little in the way of special equipment to make some impressive cakes. The equipment needed for baking cakes can be found in most kitchens: mixing bowl, sieve, weighing scales, measuring spoons and jug, wire rack and cake tins. Good-quality cake tins conduct heat evenly and efficiently for perfect results and will last for years. Since cake tin sizes vary between manufacturers, some of the recipes in this book state the tin's capacity. To find a tin's capacity, simply use a measuring jug to pour water into the tin and note how much liquid it takes to fill the tin.

Follow the top tips on the opposite page to ensure perfect results and you'll soon realize there is no time like the present to dig out your apron, get baking and rediscover the joy of an afternoon's cake-making!

• Turn on the oven before you start in order to preheat it to the correct temperature while you're mixing.

• Brush cake tins with melted butter or oil and line with non-stick baking paper to prevent sticking.

• Always use eggs at room temperature. If you store eggs in the refrigerator, remove them about 30 minutes before use to allow them to come up to room temperature.

• Avoid over-mixing because this can cause a heavy texture – beat the mixture until just smooth.

• Bake the cake immediately once mixed because the raising agents begin to act as soon as they're combined with liquid.

• Avoid opening the oven during cooking – this reduces the oven temperature and can cause cakes to sink.

• Test cakes are fully cooked – they should be well risen and starting to shrink from the sides of the tin. Sponge cakes should feel springy to the touch.

Everyday Cakes

Vanilla Victoria Sponge Cake

serves 6–8

oil or melted butter, for greasing

175 g/6 oz plain flour

1 tbsp baking powder

175 g/6 oz unsalted butter, softened

175 g/6 oz golden caster sugar

3 eggs, beaten

1 tsp vanilla extract

2 tbsp milk

filling

55 g/2 oz unsalted butter, softened

115 g/4 oz icing sugar, plus extra for dusting

½ tsp vanilla extract

3 tbsp strawberry jam

Preheat the oven to 180°C/350°F/Gas Mark 4. Grease two 20-cm/8-inch sandwich cake tins and line the bases with baking paper.

Sift the flour and baking powder into a large bowl and add the butter, caster sugar, eggs and vanilla extract. Beat well until the mixture is smooth, then stir in the milk.

Divide the mixture between the prepared tins and smooth level. Bake in the preheated oven for 25–30 minutes, or until risen, firm and golden brown. Leave to cool in the tins for 2–3 minutes, then turn out onto a wire rack to finish cooling.

For the filling, beat together the butter, icing sugar and vanilla extract until smooth. Spread this mixture on top of one of the cakes and spread the bottom of the other cake with the jam, then sandwich the two together to enclose the filling, pressing down lightly. Sprinkle with icing sugar before serving.

Angel Food Cake

serves 10

oil or melted
butter, for greasing
115 g/4 oz plain flour,
plus extra for dusting
8 large egg whites
1 tsp cream of tartar
1 tsp almond essence
250 g/9 oz caster sugar

topping
250 g/9 oz summer berries
1 tbsp lemon juice
2 tbsp icing sugar

Preheat the oven to 160°C/325°F/Gas Mark 3. Brush the inside of a 1.7-litre/3-pint ring tin with oil and dust lightly with flour.

In a clean, grease-free bowl, whisk the egg whites until they hold soft peaks. Add the cream of tartar and whisk again until the whites are stiff but not dry.

Whisk in the almond essence, then add the caster sugar, a tablespoon at a time, whisking hard between each addition. Sift in the flour and fold in lightly and evenly using a large metal spoon.

Spoon the mixture into the prepared cake tin and tap on the work surface to remove any large air bubbles. Bake in the preheated oven for 40–45 minutes, or until golden brown and firm to the touch.

Run the tip of a small knife around the edges of the cake to loosen from the tin. Leave to cool in the tin for 10 minutes, then turn out onto a wire rack to finish cooling.

For the topping, place the berries, lemon juice and icing sugar in a saucepan and heat gently until the icing sugar has dissolved. Place on top of the cake.

Frosted Carrot Cake

serves 16

oil or melted butter, for greasing

175 ml/6 fl oz sunflower oil

175 g/6 oz light muscovado sugar

3 eggs, beaten

175 g/6 oz grated carrots

85 g/3 oz sultanas

55 g/2 oz walnut pieces

grated rind of 1 orange

175 g/6 oz self-raising flour

1 tsp bicarbonate of soda

1 tsp ground cinnamon

½ tsp grated nutmeg

strips of orange zest, to decorate

frosting

200 g/7 oz full-fat soft cheese

100 g/3½ oz icing sugar

2 tsp orange juice

Preheat the oven to 180°C/350°F/Gas Mark 4. Grease a 23-cm/9-inch square cake tin and line the base with baking paper.

In a large bowl beat together the oil, muscovado sugar and eggs. Stir in the grated carrots, sultanas, walnuts and orange rind.

Sift together the flour, bicarbonate of soda, cinnamon and nutmeg, then stir evenly into the carrot mixture.

Spoon the mixture into the prepared cake tin and bake in the preheated oven for 40–45 minutes, until well risen and firm to the touch. Leave to cool in the tin for 5 minutes, then turn out onto a wire rack to finish cooling.

For the frosting, combine the soft cheese, icing sugar and orange juice in a bowl and beat until smooth. Spread over the top of the cake and swirl with a palette knife. Decorate with strips of orange zest and serve cut into squares.

14

Lemon Drizzle Cake

serves 8

oil or melted butter,
for greasing
200 g/7 oz plain flour
2 tsp baking powder
200 g/7 oz caster sugar
4 eggs
150 ml/5 fl oz soured cream
grated rind of 1 large lemon
4 tbsp lemon juice
150 ml/5 fl oz sunflower oil

syrup
4 tbsp icing sugar
3 tbsp lemon juice

Preheat the oven to 180°C/350°F/Gas Mark 4. Lightly grease a 20-cm/8-inch loose-based round cake tin and line the base with baking paper.

Sift the flour and baking powder into a mixing bowl and stir in the caster sugar. In a separate bowl, whisk the eggs, soured cream, lemon rind, lemon juice and oil together. Pour the egg mixture into the dry ingredients and mix well until evenly combined.

Pour the mixture into the prepared tin and bake in the preheated oven for 45–60 minutes, until risen and golden brown.

For the syrup, mix together the icing sugar and lemon juice in a small saucepan. Stir over a low heat until just beginning to bubble and turn syrupy.

As soon as the cake comes out of the oven, prick the surface with a fine skewer, then brush the syrup over the top. Leave the cake to cool completely in the tin before turning out and serving.

Hummingbird Cake

serves 10

oil or melted butter,
for greasing

250 g/9 oz plain flour

250 g/9 oz caster sugar

1 tsp ground cinnamon

1 tsp bicarbonate of soda

3 eggs, beaten

200 ml/7 fl oz sunflower oil

100 g/3½ oz pecan nuts,
roughly chopped,
plus extra to decorate

3 ripe bananas (about
375 g/13 oz peeled
weight), mashed

85 g/3 oz canned crushed
pineapple (drained weight),
plus 4 tbsp juice from the can

filling and frosting

175 g/6 oz full-fat soft cheese

55 g/2 oz unsalted butter

1 tsp vanilla extract

400 g/14 oz icing sugar

Preheat the oven to 180°C/350°F/Gas Mark 4. Lightly grease three 23-cm/9-inch sandwich cake tins and line the bases with baking paper.

Sift together the flour, caster sugar, cinnamon and bicarbonate of soda into a large bowl. Add the eggs, oil, pecan nuts, bananas, pineapple and pineapple juice, and stir with a wooden spoon until evenly mixed.

Divide the mixture between the prepared tins and smooth level. Bake in the preheated oven for 25–30 minutes, or until golden brown and firm to the touch.

Remove the cakes from the oven and leave to cool in the tins for 10 minutes, then turn out onto wire racks to finish cooling.

For the filling and frosting, beat together the soft cheese, butter and vanilla extract in a bowl until smooth. Sift in the icing sugar and mix until smooth.

Sandwich the cakes together with half of the mixture, spread the remaining frosting over the top, then sprinkle with pecan nuts to decorate.

Classic Cherry Cake

serves 8

oil or melted butter, for greasing
250 g/9 oz glacé cherries, quartered
85 g/3 oz ground almonds
200 g/7 oz plain flour
1 tsp baking powder
200 g/7 oz unsalted butter
200 g/7 oz caster sugar
3 large eggs
finely grated rind and juice of 1 lemon
6 sugar cubes, crushed

Preheat the oven to 180°C/350°F/Gas Mark 4. Grease a 20-cm/ 8-inch round cake tin and line with baking paper.

Stir together the cherries, ground almonds and 1 tablespoon of the flour. Sift the remaining flour into a separate bowl with the baking powder.

Cream together the butter and caster sugar until light in colour and fluffy in texture. Gradually add the eggs, beating hard with each addition, until evenly mixed.

Add the flour mixture and fold lightly and evenly into the creamed mixture with a metal spoon. Add the cherry mixture and fold in evenly. Finally, fold in the lemon rind and juice.

Spoon the mixture into the prepared cake tin and sprinkle with the crushed sugar cubes. Bake in the preheated oven for 1–1¼ hours, or until risen, golden brown and the cake is just beginning to shrink away from the sides of the tin.

Leave to cool in the tin for 15 minutes, then turn out onto a wire rack to finish cooling.

Rich Fruit Cake

serves 16

350 g/12 oz sultanas

225 g/8 oz raisins

115 g/4 oz ready-to-eat dried apricots, chopped

85 g/3 oz stoned dates, chopped

4 tbsp dark rum or brandy, plus extra for flavouring (optional)

finely grated rind and juice of 1 orange

oil or melted butter, for greasing

225 g/8 oz unsalted butter

225 g/8 oz light muscovado sugar

4 eggs

70 g/2½ oz chopped mixed peel

85 g/3 oz glacé cherries, quartered

25 g/1 oz chopped glacé ginger or stem ginger

40 g/1½ oz blanched almonds, chopped

200 g/7 oz plain flour

1 tsp ground mixed spice

Place the sultanas, raisins, apricots and dates in a large bowl and stir in the rum, orange rind and orange juice. Cover and leave to soak for several hours or overnight.

Preheat the oven to 150°C/300°F/Gas Mark 2. Grease a 20-cm/8-inch round deep cake tin and line the base with baking paper.

Cream together the butter and sugar until light and fluffy. Gradually beat in the eggs, beating hard after each addition. Stir in the soaked fruits, mixed peel, glacé cherries, glacé ginger and blanched almonds.

Sift together the flour and mixed spice, then fold lightly and evenly into the mixture. Spoon the mixture into the prepared cake tin and level the surface, making a slight depression in the centre with the back of the spoon.

Bake in the preheated oven for 2¼–2¾ hours, or until the cake is beginning to shrink away from the sides and a skewer inserted into the centre comes out clean. Cool completely in the tin.

Turn out the cake and remove the lining paper. Wrap in greaseproof paper and foil, and store for at least two months before use. To add a richer flavour, prick the cake with a skewer and spoon over a couple of extra tablespoons of rum or brandy, if using, before storing.

Coffee & Walnut Cake

serves 8

oil or melted butter,
for greasing
175 g/6 oz unsalted butter
175 g/6 oz light
muscovado sugar
3 large eggs, beaten
3 tbsp strong black coffee
175 g/6 oz self-raising flour
1½ tsp baking powder
115 g/4 oz walnut pieces
walnut halves, to decorate

filling and frosting
115 g/4 oz unsalted butter
200 g/7 oz icing sugar
1 tbsp strong black coffee
½ tsp vanilla extract

Preheat the oven to 180°C/350°F/Gas Mark 4. Grease two 20-cm/ 8-inch sandwich cake tins and line the bases with baking paper.

Cream together the butter and muscovado sugar until pale and fluffy. Gradually add the eggs, beating well after each addition. Beat in the coffee.

Sift the flour and baking powder into the mixture, then fold in lightly and evenly with a metal spoon. Fold in the walnut pieces.

Divide the mixture between the prepared cake tins and smooth level. Bake in the preheated oven for 20–25 minutes, or until golden brown and springy to the touch. Leave to cool in the tins for 5 minutes, then turn out onto a wire rack to finish cooling.

For the filling and frosting, beat together the butter, icing sugar, coffee and vanilla extract, mixing until smooth and creamy.

Use about half the mixture to sandwich the cakes together, then spread the remaining buttercream mixture on top and swirl with a palette knife. Decorate with walnut halves.

Chocolate Fudge Cake

serves 8

oil or melted butter, for greasing

55 g/2 oz plain chocolate

2 tbsp milk

175 g/6 oz plain flour

1 tbsp baking powder

175 g/6 oz unsalted butter, softened

175 g/6 oz dark muscovado sugar

3 eggs, beaten

1 tsp vanilla extract

chocolate curls or grated chocolate, to decorate

filling and frosting

100 g/3½ oz plain chocolate

55 g/2 oz unsalted butter, softened

175 g/6 oz icing sugar

1 tsp vanilla extract

1 tbsp milk

Preheat the oven to 180°C/350°F/Gas Mark 4. Grease a 23-cm/ 9-inch round cake tin and line with baking paper.

Place the chocolate and milk in a small pan and heat gently until melted, without boiling. Remove from the heat.

Sift the flour and baking powder into a large bowl and add the butter, muscovado sugar, eggs and vanilla extract. Beat well until smooth, then stir in the melted chocolate mixture, mixing evenly.

Spoon the mixture into the prepared tin and smooth level. Bake in the preheated oven for 50–60 minutes, until firm to the touch and just beginning to shrink away from the sides of the tin.

Leave to cool in the tin for 10 minutes, then turn out onto a wire rack to finish cooling. When cold, carefully slice the cake horizontally into two layers.

For the filling and frosting, melt the chocolate with the butter in a small pan over a low heat. Remove from the heat and stir in the icing sugar, vanilla extract and milk, then beat well until smooth.

Sandwich the cake layers together with half the chocolate mixture, then spread the remainder on top of the cake, swirling with a palette knife. Sprinkle with chocolate curls.

Chocolate Sandwich Cake

serves 8

oil or melted butter, for greasing

150 g/5½ oz plain flour

2 tbsp cocoa powder

1 tbsp baking powder

175 g/6 oz unsalted butter, softened

175 g/6 oz golden caster sugar

3 eggs, beaten

1 tsp vanilla extract

2 tbsp milk

140 g/5 oz chocolate spread

icing sugar, for dusting

Preheat the oven to 180°C/350°F/Gas Mark 4. Grease two 20-cm/8-inch sandwich cake tins and line the bases with baking paper.

Sift the flour, cocoa and baking powder into a large bowl and add the butter, caster sugar, eggs and vanilla extract. Beat well until the mixture is smooth, then stir in the milk.

Divide the mixture between the prepared tins and smooth level. Bake in the preheated oven for 25–30 minutes, or until well risen and firm to the touch. Leave to cool in the tins for 2–3 minutes, then turn out onto a wire rack to finish cooling.

When the cakes have cooled completely, sandwich together with the chocolate spread, then dust with icing sugar and serve.

Celebration Cakes

Dotty Chocolate Chip Cake

serves 10

oil or melted butter,
for greasing
175 g/6 oz soft margarine
175 g/6 oz caster sugar
3 eggs, beaten
175 g/6 oz plain flour
1 tsp baking powder
2 tbsp cocoa powder
55 g/2 oz white
chocolate chips
40 g/1½ oz small coloured
sweets, to decorate

icing
175 g/6 oz milk chocolate or
plain chocolate
100 g/3½ oz unsalted
butter or margarine
1 tbsp golden syrup

Preheat the oven to 160°C/325°F/Gas Mark 3. Grease a 20-cm/ 8-inch round cake tin and line the base with baking paper.

Place the margarine, sugar, eggs, flour, baking powder and cocoa powder in a bowl and beat until just smooth. Stir in the chocolate chips, mixing evenly.

Spoon the mixture into the prepared tins and smooth level. Bake in the preheated oven for 40–45 minutes, until risen and firm to the touch. Leave to cool in the tins for 5 minutes, then turn out onto a wire rack to finish cooling.

For the icing, place the chocolate, butter and golden syrup in a saucepan over a low heat and stir until just melted and smooth.

Remove from the heat and leave to cool until it begins to thicken enough to leave a trail when the spoon is lifted. Pour the icing over the top of the cake, allowing it to drizzle down the sides. Arrange the sweets over the top of the cake.

Birthday Lemon Sponge Cake

serves 8–10

oil or melted butter,
for greasing
250 g/9 oz unsalted butter,
250 g/9 oz golden caster
sugar
4 eggs, beaten
250 g/9 oz self-raising flour
finely grated rind of 1 lemon
3 tbsp milk

filling and frosting
140 g/5 oz unsalted butter
200 g/7 oz icing sugar
2 tbsp lemon juice
3 tbsp lemon curd

Preheat the oven to 180°C/350°F/Gas Mark 4. Grease two 20-cm/8-inch sandwich cake tins and line the bases with baking paper.

Cream together the butter and caster sugar until pale and fluffy. Gradually add the eggs, beating well after each addition. Sift in the flour and fold in evenly with a metal spoon. Fold in the lemon rind and milk lightly and evenly.

Spoon the mixture into the prepared tins and bake in the preheated oven for 25–30 minutes, or until golden brown and springy to the touch. Leave the cakes to cool in the tins for 2–3 minutes, then turn out onto a wire rack to finish cooling.

For the frosting, beat together the butter, icing sugar and lemon juice until smooth. For the filling, mix about 3 tablespoons of the frosting with the lemon curd. Use the lemon curd mixture to sandwich the two cakes together.

Spread about two thirds of the remaining frosting over the top of the cake, swirling with a palette knife. Spoon the remainder into a piping bag and pipe swirls around the edge of the cake. Add candleholders and birthday candles to finish.

Rose Gateau

serves 8–10

oil or melted butter,
for greasing
175 g/6 oz plain flour
1 tbsp baking powder
175 g/6 oz unsalted
butter, softened
175 g/6 oz caster sugar
3 eggs, beaten
1 tsp rosewater
2 tbsp milk

filling and icing
150 ml/5 fl oz whipping
cream
1 tsp rosewater
200 g/7 oz icing sugar, sifted

to decorate
fresh rose petals, washed
and patted dry
½ egg white
caster sugar, for sprinkling

Preheat the oven to 180°C/350°F/Gas Mark 4. Grease two 23-cm/9-inch sandwich cake tins and line the bases with baking paper.

Sift the flour and baking powder into a large bowl and add the butter, caster sugar, eggs and rosewater. Beat well until the mixture is smooth, then stir in the milk.

Divide the mixture between the prepared tins and smooth. Bake in the preheated oven for 25–30 minutes, or until risen, firm and golden brown. Leave to cool in the tins for 2–3 minutes, then turn out onto a wire rack to finish cooling.

For the filling, whip the cream with ½ teaspoon of the rosewater until just thick enough to hold its shape. Use to sandwich the cakes together.

For the icing, mix the icing sugar with the remaining rosewater and just enough water to mix to a thick pouring consistency. Spoon over the cake, allowing it to drizzle down the sides. Leave to set.

Brush the rose petals with the egg white, sprinkle with caster sugar and arrange on top of the cake to decorate.

Marbled Pastel Cake

serves 12

oil or melted butter,
for greasing
175 g/6 oz plain flour
1 tbsp baking powder
175 g/6 oz unsalted
butter, softened
175 g/6 oz caster sugar
3 eggs, beaten
1 tsp vanilla extract
2 tbsp milk
pink edible food colouring
700 g/1 lb 9 oz ready-to-
roll soft icing
3 tbsp apricot jam, warmed
sugar flowers, to decorate

Preheat the oven to 160°C/325°F/Gas Mark 3. Grease a 23-cm/
9-inch round deep cake tin and line with baking paper.

Sift the flour and baking powder into a large bowl and add the
butter, sugar, eggs and vanilla extract. Beat well until the mixture
is smooth, then stir in the milk. Spoon half the mixture into a
separate bowl and stir in a few drops of pink food colouring.

Spoon alternate tablespoonfuls of the two mixtures into
the prepared tin and swirl lightly with a palette knife for a
marbled effect.

Bake in the preheated oven for 40–50 minutes, or until risen, firm
and golden brown. Leave to cool in the tin for 10 minutes, then
turn out onto a wire rack to finish cooling.

Divide the icing into two halves and knead a little pink food
colouring into one half. Knead the pink and white icing together
for a marbled effect.

Place the cake on a board, brush with apricot jam and roll out the
icing to cover the cake. Trim the edges, then roll out the trimmings
into two long ropes, twist together and place around the base of
the cake. Decorate with sugar flowers.

Bumblebee Cake

serves 8–10

oil or melted butter,
for greasing
235 g/8½ oz plain flour
1 tbsp baking powder
175 g/6 oz unsalted
butter, softened
175 g/6 oz caster sugar
3 eggs, beaten
1 tsp vanilla extract
2 tbsp lemon juice
finely grated rind of 1 lemon

filling and frosting
175 g/6 oz unsalted butter
250 g/9 oz icing sugar, sifted
3 tbsp clear honey
2 tbsp lemon juice

to decorate
250 g/9 oz white ready-
to-roll icing
a few drops of yellow and
black edible food colouring

Preheat the oven to 160°C/325°F/Gas Mark 3. Grease a
1.5-litre/2¾-pint ovenproof pudding basin.

Sift the flour and baking powder into a bowl and add the butter,
caster sugar, eggs and vanilla extract. Beat well until smooth, then
stir in the lemon juice and rind.

Spoon the mixture into the prepared basin and smooth level. Bake
in the preheated oven for 1¼–1½ hours, or until risen, firm and
golden brown. Leave to cool in the basin for 5 minutes, then turn
out onto a wire rack to finish cooling.

For the filling and frosting, beat together the butter, icing sugar,
honey and lemon juice until smooth. Slice the cake horizontally
into three layers. Use about a quarter of the buttercream mixture
to sandwich the layers together.

Using a piping bag with a large plain nozzle, pipe the remaining
mixture in lines around the cake to resemble a beehive.

Reserve a quarter of the white icing, then colour half the
remainder yellow and half black. Shape to make small bees,
making the wings from the white icing and fixing with a dab
of water. Press the bees into the frosting.

Valentine Chocolate Heart Cake

serves 12

oil or melted butter,
for greasing
175 g/6 oz self-raising flour
2 tsp baking powder
55 g/2 oz cocoa powder
3 eggs
140 g/5 oz light
muscovado sugar
150 ml/5 fl oz sunflower oil
150 ml/5 fl oz single cream
fresh mint sprigs, to decorate

filling and topping
225 g/8 oz plain chocolate
250 ml/9 fl oz double cream
3 tbsp seedless raspberry jam
200 g/7 oz fresh or
frozen raspberries

Preheat the oven to 180°C/350°F/Gas Mark 4. Grease a 20-cm/
8-inch heart-shaped cake tin and line the base with baking paper.

Sift the flour, baking powder and cocoa powder into a large bowl.
Beat the eggs with the sugar, oil and single cream. Make a well
in the dry ingredients and add the egg mixture, then stir to mix
thoroughly, beating to a smooth batter.

Pour the mixture into the prepared tin and bake in the preheated
oven for 25–30 minutes, or until risen and firm to the touch. Leave
to cool in the tin for 10 minutes, then turn out and finish cooling
on a wire rack.

For the filling and topping, place the chocolate and double
cream in a saucepan over a low heat and stir until melted.
Remove from the heat and stir until the mixture cools slightly
and begins to thicken.

Use a sharp knife to cut the cake in half horizontally. Spread the
cut surface of each half with the raspberry jam, then top with
about 3 tablespoons of the chocolate mixture. Scatter half the
raspberries over the base and replace the top, pressing lightly.

Spread the remaining chocolate mixture over the top and sides
of the cake, swirling with a palette knife. Top with the remaining
raspberries and decorate with mint sprigs.

Easter Simnel Cake

serves 16

oil or melted butter,
for greasing
175 g/6 oz unsalted butter
175 g/6 oz light
muscovado sugar
3 eggs, beaten
225 g/8 oz plain flour
½ tsp baking powder
2 tsp ground mixed spice
finely grated rind of
1 small lemon
100 g/3½ oz currants
100 g/3½ oz sultanas
55 g/2 oz chopped mixed peel
700 g/1 lb 9 oz marzipan
3 tbsp apricot jam

Preheat the oven to 150°C/300°F/Gas Mark 2. Grease and line a 20-cm/8-inch round deep cake tin with baking paper.

Place the butter and sugar in a bowl and cream together until pale, light and fluffy. Gradually beat in the eggs, beating hard after each addition. Sift together the flour, baking powder and mixed spice. Use a large metal spoon to fold into the creamed mixture. Stir in the lemon rind, currants, sultanas and mixed peel, mixing evenly. Spoon half the mixture into the prepared tin and smooth level.

Roll out 250 g/9 oz of the marzipan to a 20-cm/8-inch round and place over the mixture in the tin. Add the remaining cake mixture and smooth level. Bake the cake in the preheated oven for 2¼–2¾ hours, or until firm and golden and the sides are beginning to shrink away from the tin. Leave to cool in the tin for 30 minutes, then turn out onto a wire rack to finish cooling.

Brush the top of the cake with apricot jam. Roll out two thirds of the remaining marzipan to a round to cover the top of the cake. Use a knife to mark a lattice design in the surface and pinch the edges to decorate.

Roll the remaining marzipan into 11 small balls and arrange around the edge of the cake. Place under a hot grill for 30–40 seconds to brown lightly. Cool before storing.

Halloween Pumpkin Cake

serves 10

oil or melted butter,
for greasing
175 g/6 oz plain flour
1 tbsp baking powder
1 tsp ground mixed spice
175 g/6 oz unsalted
butter, softened
175 g/6 oz light
muscovado sugar
3 eggs, beaten
1 tsp vanilla extract
175 g/6 oz pumpkin flesh,
coarsely grated

to decorate
3 tbsp apricot jam, warmed
a few drops of orange and
black edible food colouring
800 g/1 lb 12 oz ready-to-roll
soft icing
black, green and yellow
writing icing

Preheat the oven to 160°C/325°F/Gas Mark 3. Grease a 23-cm/9-inch round deep cake tin and line with baking paper.

Sift the flour, baking powder and mixed spice into a bowl and add the butter, sugar, eggs and vanilla extract. Beat well until smooth, then stir in the pumpkin.

Spoon the mixture into the prepared tin and smooth level. Bake in the preheated oven for 40–50 minutes, or until risen, firm and golden brown. Leave to cool in the tin for 10 minutes, then turn out onto a wire rack to finish cooling.

Brush the cake with warmed apricot jam. Knead orange food colouring into about three quarters of the icing and roll out to cover the top and sides of the cake. Trim the edges neatly, reserving the trimmings.

Form the trimmings into small pumpkin shapes and use the black writing icing to pipe faces and the green writing icing to pipe stalks onto them. Knead black food colouring into the remaining icing, then roll it out and cut into bat shapes. Pipe eyes onto the bats using yellow writing icing, then place the bats and the pumpkins onto the cake to decorate.

Golden Christmas Cake

serves 16–18

175 g/6 oz dried apricots, chopped

85 g/3 oz dried mango, chopped

85 g/3 oz dried pineapple, chopped

175 g/6 oz sultanas

55 g/2 oz chopped stem ginger

55 g/2 oz chopped mixed peel

finely grated rind and juice of 1 orange

4 tbsp brandy

oil or melted butter, for greasing

175 g/6 oz unsalted butter

100 g/3½ oz light muscovado sugar

4 eggs, beaten

2 tbsp clear honey

175 g/6 oz self-raising flour

2 tsp ground allspice

85 g/3 oz pecan nuts

to decorate (optional)
800 g/1 lb 12 oz marzipan

900 g/2 lb ready-to-roll icing

silver dragées

Place the chopped apricots, mango and pineapple in a bowl with the sultanas, stem ginger and mixed peel. Stir in the orange rind, orange juice and brandy. Cover the bowl and leave to soak overnight.

Preheat the oven to 170°C/325°F/Gas Mark 3. Grease a 23-cm/ 9-inch round springform cake tin and line with baking paper.

Cream together the butter and sugar until the mixture is pale and fluffy. Add the eggs to the mixture, beating well between each addition. Stir in the honey.

Sift the flour with the allspice and fold into the mixture using a metal spoon. Add the soaked fruit and pecan nuts, stirring thoroughly to mix. Spoon the mixture into the prepared tin, spreading evenly, then make a slight dip in the centre.

Place the tin in the centre of the preheated oven and bake for 1½–2 hours, or until golden brown and firm to the touch and a skewer inserted into the centre comes out clean. Leave to cool in the tin.

Turn the cake out, remove the lining paper and re-wrap in clean baking paper and foil. Store in a cool place for at least 1 month before use. If desired, cover the cake with marzipan and ready-to-roll icing, following the pack instructions, and decorate with silver dragées.

Christmas Mulled Sponge Loaf

serves 8

oil or melted butter,
for greasing
175 g/6 oz plain flour
1 tbsp baking powder
1 tsp ground mixed spice
175 g/6 oz unsalted
butter, softened
175 g/6 oz light
muscovado sugar
3 eggs, beaten
1 tsp vanilla extract
finely grated rind of 1 orange
2 tbsp orange juice

syrup
70 g/2½ oz icing sugar
100 ml/3½ fl oz port or
red wine
1 piece star anise

to decorate
10 fresh cranberries
10 fresh bay leaves
1 egg white
caster sugar, for sprinkling

Preheat the oven to 180°C/350°F/Gas Mark 4. Grease a 1.2-litre/2-pint loaf tin and line with baking paper.

Sift the flour, baking powder and mixed spice into a large bowl and add the butter, muscovado sugar, eggs and vanilla extract. Beat well until the mixture is smooth, then stir in the orange rind and juice.

Spoon the mixture into the prepared tin and smooth level. Bake in the preheated oven for 40–50 minutes, or until risen, firm and golden brown. (Don't worry if the cake dips slightly in the centre.)

Remove the tin from the oven and stand it on a wire rack. To make the syrup, place the icing sugar, port and star anise in a pan and heat gently until boiling. Boil rapidly for 2–3 minutes to reduce slightly. Remove and discard the star anise.

Spoon the syrup over the cake and leave to soak for 30 minutes. Turn out the cake from the tin, upside down.

Brush the cranberries and bay leaves with egg white and sprinkle with caster sugar, then arrange on top of the cake.

Something Different

Caribbean Coconut Cake

serves 10

oil or melted butter,
for greasing
175 g/6 oz butter, softened
175 g/6 oz golden
caster sugar
3 eggs
175 g/6 oz self-raising flour
1½ tsp baking powder
½ tsp freshly grated nutmeg
55 g/2 oz desiccated coconut
2 tbsp coconut cream
toasted desiccated coconut,
to decorate

filling and frosting
280 g/10 oz icing sugar
115 g/4 oz butter
3 tbsp coconut cream
5 tbsp pineapple jam

Preheat the oven to 180°C/350°F/Gas Mark 4. Grease two 20-cm/ 8-inch sandwich cake tins and line the bases with baking paper.

Place the butter in a bowl with the caster sugar and eggs and sift in the flour, baking powder and nutmeg. Beat together until smooth, then stir in the desiccated coconut and the coconut cream.

Divide the mixture between the prepared tins and smooth level. Bake in the preheated oven for 25 minutes, or until golden and firm to the touch. Leave to cool in the tins for 5 minutes, then turn out onto a wire rack to finish cooling.

For the filling and frosting, sift the icing sugar into a bowl and add the butter and coconut cream. Beat together until smooth. Spread the pineapple jam on one of the cakes and top with just under half of the buttercream. Place the other cake on top. Spread the remaining buttercream on top of the cake and scatter with toasted desiccated coconut.

Pineapple Upside-down Cake

serves 10

oil or melted butter,
for greasing
4 eggs, beaten
200 g/7 oz golden caster
sugar
1 tsp vanilla extract
200 g/7 oz plain flour
2 tsp baking powder
125 g/4½ oz unsalted
butter, melted

topping
40 g/1½ oz unsalted butter
4 tbsp golden syrup
425 g/15 oz canned pineapple
rings, drained
4–6 glacé cherries, halved

Preheat the oven to 160°C/325°F/Gas Mark 3. Grease a 23-cm/9-inch round deep cake tin with a solid base and line the base with baking paper.

For the topping, place the butter and golden syrup in a heavy-based saucepan and heat gently until melted. Bring to the boil and boil for 2–3 minutes, stirring, until slightly thickened and toffee-like.

Pour the syrup into the base of the prepared tin. Arrange the pineapple rings and glacé cherries in one layer over the syrup.

Place the eggs, sugar and vanilla extract in a large heatproof bowl over a saucepan of gently simmering water and whisk with an electric mixer for about 10–15 minutes, until thick enough to leave a trail when the whisk is lifted. Sift in the flour and baking powder and fold in lightly and evenly with a metal spoon.

Fold the melted butter into the mixture with a metal spoon until evenly mixed. Spoon into the prepared tin and bake in the preheated oven for 1–1¼ hours, or until well risen, firm and golden brown.

Leave to cool in the tin for 10 minutes, then carefully turn out onto a serving plate. Serve warm or cold.

Orange & Poppy Seed Bundt Cake

serves 10

oil or melted butter,
for greasing

300 g/10½ oz plain flour,
plus extra for dusting

200 g/7 oz unsalted butter

200 g/7 oz golden caster
sugar

3 large eggs, beaten

finely grated rind of 1 orange

55 g/2 oz poppy seeds

2 tsp baking powder

150 ml/5 fl oz milk

125 ml/4 fl oz orange juice

strips of orange zest,
to decorate

syrup

140 g/5 oz golden caster
sugar

150 ml/5 fl oz orange juice

Preheat the oven to 160°C/325°F/Gas Mark 3. Grease and lightly flour a 1.7-litre/3-pint ring tin.

Cream together the butter and sugar until pale and fluffy, then add the eggs gradually, beating thoroughly after each addition. Stir in the orange rind and poppy seeds. Sift in the flour and baking powder, then fold in evenly. Add the milk and orange juice, stirring to mix evenly.

Spoon the mixture into the prepared tin and bake in the preheated oven for 45–50 minutes, or until firm and golden brown. Leave to cool in the tin for 10 minutes, then turn out onto a wire rack to finish cooling.

For the syrup, place the sugar and orange juice in a saucepan and heat gently until the sugar melts. Bring to the boil and simmer for about 5 minutes, until reduced and syrupy.

Spoon the syrup over the cake while it is still warm. Top with the strips of orange zest and serve warm or cold.

Apple Sauce Cake

serves 6

oil or melted butter,
for greasing

175 g/6 oz plain flour

1 tbsp cornflour

1 tbsp baking powder

175 g/6 oz unsalted
butter, softened

175 g/6 oz caster sugar,
plus extra for sprinkling

3 eggs, beaten

1 tsp vanilla extract

200 g/7 oz apple sauce or
thick apple purée

1 eating apple

lemon juice, for brushing

Preheat the oven to 180°C/350°F/Gas Mark 4. Grease two 20-cm/8-inch sandwich cake tins and line the bases with baking paper.

Sift the flour, cornflour and baking powder into a large bowl and add the butter, sugar, eggs and vanilla extract. Beat well until the mixture is smooth. Stir in 85 g/3 oz of the apple sauce.

Divide the mixture between the prepared tins and smooth level. Bake in the preheated oven for 25–30 minutes, or until risen, firm and golden brown.

Leave to cool in the tins for 5 minutes, then turn out onto a wire rack to finish cooling. Use the remaining apple sauce to sandwich the cakes together.

Core and thinly slice the apple and brush with lemon juice. Arrange the slices on top of the cake to decorate, then sprinkle with a little caster sugar.

Glazed Fruit & Nut Cake

serves 16–18

oil or melted butter,
for greasing

250 g/9 oz plain flour,
plus extra for dusting

1 tbsp baking powder

1 tsp ground mixed spice

175 g/6 oz unsalted
butter, softened

175 g/6 oz dark
muscovado sugar

3 eggs, beaten

1 tsp vanilla extract

2 tbsp milk

300 g/10½ oz mixed
dried fruit

85 g/3 oz chopped mixed nuts

to decorate

3 tbsp clear honey, warmed

350 g/12 oz mixed glacé
fruits, such as pineapple,
cherries and orange

55 g/2 oz whole shelled nuts,
such as Brazil nuts,
almonds and walnuts

Preheat the oven to 160°C/325°F/Gas Mark 3. Grease a 23-cm/ 9-inch round springform cake tin and sprinkle with a little flour to coat, shaking out the excess.

Sift the flour, baking powder and mixed spice into a large bowl and add the butter, sugar, eggs and vanilla extract. Beat well until the mixture is smooth, then stir in the milk, mixed dried fruit and chopped mixed nuts.

Spoon the mixture into the prepared tin and smooth level. Bake in the preheated oven for about 1 hour, or until risen, firm and golden brown.

Leave to cool in the tin for 30 minutes, then remove the sides and place on a wire rack to finish cooling.

Brush the top of the cake with a little of the warmed honey then arrange the glacé fruits and whole shelled nuts on top. Brush with the remaining honey and leave to set.

Mocha Layer Cake

serves 8

oil or melted butter,
for greasing
250 g/9 oz self-raising flour
¼ tsp baking powder
4 tbsp cocoa powder
115 g/4 oz caster sugar
2 eggs
2 tbsp golden syrup
150 ml/5 fl oz sunflower oil
150 ml/5 fl oz milk

filling and topping
1 tsp instant coffee powder
1 tbsp boiling water
300 ml/10 fl oz double cream
2 tbsp icing sugar

to decorate
50 g/1¾ oz chocolate
shavings
marbled chocolate caraque
icing sugar, for dusting

Preheat the oven to 180°C/350°F/Gas Mark 4. Grease three 18-cm/7-inch sandwich cake tins and line with baking paper.

Sift the flour, baking powder and cocoa into a large mixing bowl. Stir in the caster sugar. Make a well in the centre and stir in the eggs, syrup, oil and milk. Beat with a wooden spoon, gradually mixing in the dry ingredients to make a smooth mixture.

Divide the mixture between the prepared tins. Bake in the preheated oven for 35–45 minutes, or until springy to the touch. Leave the cakes to cool in their tins for 5 minutes, then turn out onto wire racks to finish cooling.

For the filling and topping, dissolve the instant coffee in the boiling water and place in a bowl with the cream and icing sugar. Whip until the cream is just holding its shape. Use half of the cream to sandwich the 3 cakes together. Spread the remaining cream over the top and sides of the cake.

To decorate, lightly press the chocolate shavings into the cream around the edge of the cake. Transfer to a serving plate. Lay the caraque over the top of the cake. Cut a few thin strips of baking paper and place on top of the caraque. Dust lightly with icing sugar, then carefully remove the paper.

Rich Chocolate Rum Torte

serves 8

oil or melted butter,
for greasing
70 g/2½ oz plain chocolate,
broken into pieces
2 tbsp milk
175 g/6 oz plain flour
1 tbsp baking powder
175 g/6 oz unsalted
butter, softened
175 g/6 oz dark
muscovado sugar
3 eggs, beaten
1 tsp vanilla extract
chocolate curls or grated
chocolate, to decorate

filling and frosting
225 g/8 oz plain chocolate,
broken into pieces
225 ml/8 fl oz double cream
2 tbsp dark rum

Preheat the oven to 180°C/350°F/Gas Mark 4. Grease three
18-cm/7-inch sandwich cake tins and line with baking paper.

Place the chocolate and milk in a small saucepan and heat gently,
without boiling, until melted. Stir and remove from the heat.

Sift the flour and baking powder into a large bowl and add the
butter, sugar, eggs and vanilla extract. Beat well until smooth, then
stir in the chocolate mixture.

Divide the mixture between the prepared tins and smooth level.
Bake in the preheated oven for 20–25 minutes, until risen and firm
to the touch.

Leave to cool in the tins for 5 minutes, then turn out onto wire
racks to finish cooling.

For the filling and frosting, melt the chocolate with the cream and
rum in a small saucepan over a low heat. Remove from the
heat and leave to cool, stirring occasionally, until it reaches
a spreadable consistency.

Sandwich the cakes together with about a third of the chocolate
mixture, then spread the remainder over the top and sides of the
cake, swirling with a palette knife. Sprinkle with chocolate curls
and leave to set.

Chocolate Ganache Cake

serves 10

oil or melted butter,
for greasing

175 g/6 oz butter

175 g/6 oz caster sugar

4 eggs, beaten lightly

250 g/9 oz self-raising flour

1 tbsp cocoa powder

50 g/1¾ oz plain
chocolate, melted

200 g/7 oz chocolate-
flavoured cake covering

ganache

450 ml/16 fl oz double cream

375 g/13 oz plain chocolate,
broken into pieces

Preheat the oven to 180°C/350°F/Gas Mark 4. Grease a 20-cm/ 8-inch square springform cake tin and line with baking paper.

Beat the butter and sugar until light and fluffy. Gradually add the eggs, beating well after each addition. Sift the flour and cocoa together. Fold into the cake mixture. Fold in the melted chocolate.

Pour into the prepared tin and smooth level. Bake in the preheated oven for 40 minutes, or until springy to the touch. Leave the cake to cool for 5 minutes in the tin, then turn out onto a wire rack to finish cooling. Cut the cake into 2 layers.

For the ganache, place the cream in a saucepan and bring to the boil, stirring. Add the chocolate and stir until melted. Pour into a bowl, cool, then chill for 2 hours, or until set and firm. Whisk the mixture until light and fluffy. Reserve one-third of the ganache. Use the remaining ganache to sandwich the cake together and spread over the top and sides of the cake.

Melt the cake covering and spread it over a large sheet of baking paper. Leave to cool until just set. Cut into strips a little wider than the height of the cake. Place the strips around the edge of the cake, overlapping them slightly.

Pipe the reserved ganache in tear drops or shells to cover the top of the cake. Leave to chill for 1 hour.

Chocolate & Almond Layer Cake

serves 10–12

oil or melted butter,
for greasing
7 eggs
200 g/7 oz caster sugar
150 g/5½ oz plain flour
50 g/1¾ oz cocoa powder
50 g/1¾ oz butter, melted

filling and topping
200 g/7 oz dark chocolate
125 g/4½ oz butter
50 g/1¾ oz icing sugar

to decorate
75 g/2¾ oz toasted flaked
almonds, crushed lightly
grated chocolate

Preheat the oven to 180°C/350°F/Gas Mark 4. Grease a deep 23-cm/9-inch square cake tin and line the base with baking paper.

Whisk the eggs and caster sugar in a mixing bowl with an electric whisk for about 10 minutes, or until the mixture is very light and foamy and the whisk leaves a trail that lasts a few seconds when lifted.

Sift the flour and cocoa together and fold half into the mixture. Drizzle over the melted butter and fold in the rest of the flour and cocoa. Pour into the prepared tin and bake in the preheated oven for 30–35 minutes, or until springy to the touch. Leave to cool in the tin for 5 minutes, then turn out onto a wire rack to finish cooling.

For the filling and topping, melt the chocolate and butter together, then remove from the heat. Stir in the icing sugar, leave to cool, then beat until thick enough to spread.

Halve the cake lengthways and cut each half into 3 layers. Sandwich the layers together with three quarters of the chocolate mixture. Spread the remainder over the cake and mark a wavy pattern on the top. To decorate, press the almonds onto the sides and sprinkle with the grated chocolate.

Stollen

serves 8

150 ml/5 fl oz lukewarm milk
55 g/2 oz caster sugar
2 tsp active dried yeast
350 g/12 oz strong white bread flour
½ tsp salt
115 g/4 oz butter, softened
1 medium egg, beaten
40 g/1½ oz currants
55 g/2 oz sultanas
55 g/2 oz candied peel, finely diced
55 g/2 oz glacé cherries
25 g/1 oz blanched almonds, chopped
grated rind of ½ lemon
175 g/6 oz marzipan, formed into a 23-cm/9-inch sausage
oil or melted butter, for greasing

icing
115 g/4 oz icing sugar, sifted
1 tbsp water

Pour the warm milk into a small bowl, add 1 teaspoon of the caster sugar, sprinkle over the yeast, and whisk thoroughly. Set aside for 10 minutes, until a frothy head has formed.

Set aside 2 tablespoons of flour and sift the rest into a large mixing bowl with the salt and remaining caster sugar. Make a well in the centre, pour in the yeast mixture, then add the butter and beaten egg. Mix well to form a soft dough.

Mix in the currants, sultanas, peel, cherries, almonds and lemon rind, then transfer the dough to a counter and knead for 5 minutes, until smooth and elastic. Place in a clean bowl, cover with clingfilm and stand in a warm place for 1½–2 hours, until doubled in size.

Sprinkle the reserved flour onto a work surface and turn out the dough onto it. Punch out the air, then knead again until smooth and elastic. Roll out to a 25 x 20-cm/10 x 8-inch rectangle and place the marzipan in the centre. Grease a baking sheet. Fold the dough over the marzipan and place, seam-side down, on the prepared baking sheet. Cover and set aside until doubled in size. Meanwhile, preheat the oven to 190°C/375°F/Gas Mark 5.

Bake in the preheated oven for 35–40 minutes, until risen and golden. Transfer to a wire rack to cool slightly. Mix the icing sugar with the water and spread it thinly over the stollen while it is still warm. Cut into slices and serve.

Dessert Cakes

New York Cheesecake

serves 10

100 g/3½ oz butter

150 g/5½ oz digestive biscuits, finely crushed

1 tbsp granulated sugar

900 g/2 lb cream cheese

250 g/9 oz caster sugar

2 tbsp plain flour

1 tsp vanilla extract

finely grated zest of 1 orange

finely grated zest of 1 lemon

3 eggs

2 egg yolks

300 ml/10 fl oz double cream

oil or melted butter, for greasing

Preheat the oven to 180°C/350°F/Gas Mark 4. Place a small saucepan over a low heat, add the butter and heat until it melts, then remove from the heat, stir in the crushed biscuits and granulated sugar and mix throughly. Press the biscuit mixture tightly into the base of a 23-cm/9-inch round springform cake tin. Bake in the preheated oven for 10 minutes. Remove from the oven and leave to cool on a wire rack.

Increase the oven temperature to 200°C/400°F/Gas Mark 6. In an electric food mixer beat the cream cheese until creamy, then gradually add the caster sugar and flour and beat until smooth. Increase the speed and beat in the vanilla extract, orange zest and lemon zest, then beat in the eggs and egg yolks one at a time. Finally, beat in the cream. Scrape any excess from the sides and paddles of the beater into the mixture. It should be light and whippy – beat on a faster setting if you need to.

Grease the sides of the cake tin and pour in the filling. Smooth the top, transfer to the preheated oven and bake for 15 minutes, then reduce the temperature to 110°C/225°F/Gas Mark ¼ and bake for a further 30 minutes. Turn off the oven and leave the cheesecake in it for 2 hours to cool and set. Cover and refrigerate overnight.

Orange Cheesecake Gateau

serves 8–10

oil or melted butter,
for greasing
175 g/6 oz plain flour
1 tbsp baking powder
175 g/6 oz unsalted butter,
softened
175 g/6 oz golden caster
sugar
3 eggs, beaten
1 tsp orange flower water
2 tbsp orange juice

filling and topping
600 g/1 lb 5 oz
mascarpone cheese
finely grated rind of 1 orange
4 tbsp orange juice
55 g/2 oz icing sugar
1 tsp orange flower water

decorate
1 orange, peeled and sliced
maple syrup, for brushing

Preheat the oven to 180°C/350°F/Gas Mark 4. Grease two 23-cm/9-inch sandwich cake tins and line with baking paper.

Sift the flour and baking powder into a large bowl and add the butter, caster sugar, eggs and orange flower water. Beat well until the mixture is smooth, then stir in the orange juice.

Spoon the mixture into the prepared tins and smooth level. Bake in the preheated oven for 25–30 minutes, or until risen and golden brown. Leave to cool in the tins for 5 minutes, then turn out onto a wire rack to finish cooling.

For the filling and topping, beat together all of the ingredients until smooth, then spread about a third over one cake. Spoon the remainder into a piping bag fitted with a large star nozzle and pipe swirls around the edge of the cake.

Place the second cake on top. Pipe the remaining topping around the top edge. Fill the centre with orange slices and brush with maple syrup.

Citrus Mousse Cake

serves 12

oil or melted butter,
for greasing

175 g/6 oz butter

175 g/6 oz caster sugar

4 eggs, lightly beaten

200 g/7 oz self-raising flour

1 tbsp cocoa powder

50 g/1¾ oz orange-flavoured
plain chocolate, melted

peeled orange segments,
to decorate

filling and topping

2 eggs, separated

50 g/1¾ oz caster sugar

200 ml/7 fl oz freshly
squeezed orange juice

2 tsp powdered gelatine

3 tbsp water

300 ml/10 fl oz double cream

Preheat the oven to 180°C/350°F/Gas Mark 4. Grease a 20-cm/ 8-inch round springform cake tin and and line the base with baking paper.

Beat the butter and sugar in a bowl until light and fluffy. Gradually add the eggs, beating well after each addition. Sift together the flour and cocoa and fold into the creamed mixture. Fold in the melted chocolate. Pour into the prepared tin and smooth level. Bake in the preheated oven for 40 minutes, or until springy to the touch. Leave to cool for 5 minutes in the tin, then turn out onto a wire rack to finish cooling. Cut the cold cake horizontally and place one half back into the cake tin.

For the filling, beat the egg yolks and sugar until pale, then whisk in the orange juice. Sprinkle the gelatine over the water in a small bowl and allow to go spongy, then place over a saucepan of hot water and stir until dissolved. Stir into the egg yolk mixture.

Whip the cream until holding its shape, reserve a little for the topping and fold the rest into the mousse. Whisk the egg whites until standing in soft peaks, then fold in. Leave in a cool place until starting to set, stirring occasionally.

Pour the mixture into the tin and place the second half of the cake on top. Chill in the refrigerator until set. Turn out the cake, pipe teaspoonfuls of cream around the top and decorate the centre with orange segments.

Strawberry Mousse Cake

serves 8–10

oil or melted butter,
for greasing
175 g/6 oz plain flour
1 tbsp baking powder
175 g/6 oz unsalted
butter, softened
175 g/6 oz golden caster
sugar
3 eggs, beaten
1 tsp vanilla extract
2 tbsp milk

filling and topping
4 tsp powdered gelatine
3 tbsp orange juice
550 g/1 lb 4 oz fresh
strawberries
3 tbsp golden caster sugar
400 ml/14 fl oz double cream
100 g/3½ oz redcurrant
jelly, warmed

Preheat the oven to 160°C/325°F/Gas Mark 3. Grease a 23-cm/ 9-inch round springform cake tin and line with baking paper.

Sift the flour and baking powder into a large bowl and add the butter, sugar, eggs and vanilla extract. Beat well until the mixture is smooth, then stir in the milk.

Spoon the mixture into the prepared tin and smooth level. Bake in the preheated oven for 45–55 minutes, or until risen, firm and golden brown.

Leave to cool in the tin for 5 minutes, then turn out onto a wire rack to finish cooling. Cut the sponge in half horizontally and place one half back in the cake tin.

For the filling, dissolve the gelatine in the orange juice in a small bowl placed in a saucepan of hot water. In a blender or processor, purée 400 g/14 oz of the strawberries with the sugar. Whip the cream until thick enough to hold its shape. Quickly stir the gelatine mixture into the strawberry mixture, then fold in the cream.

Pour the mixture into the tin and place the second half of the cake on top. Chill in the refrigerator until set. Turn out the cake and spread the top with the warmed redcurrant jelly. Decorate with the remaining strawberries.

Meringue-topped Coffee Liqueur Cake

serves 6–8

oil or melted butter,
for greasing
175 g/6 oz plain flour
1 tbsp baking powder
175 g/6 oz unsalted butter,
softened
175 g/6 oz light
muscovado sugar
3 eggs, beaten
1 tsp coffee extract
2 tbsp milk
3 tbsp coffee liqueur

meringue topping
3 egg whites
150 g/5½ oz caster sugar
1½ tsp coffee extract

Preheat the oven to 160°C/325°F/Gas Mark 3. Grease a 25-cm/
10-inch round cake tin and line with baking paper.

Sift the flour and baking powder into a large bowl and add the
butter, muscovado sugar, eggs and coffee extract. Beat well until
the mixture is smooth, then stir in the milk.

Spoon the mixture into the prepared tin and smooth level. Bake
in the preheated oven for 40–50 minutes, or until risen, firm and
golden brown.

Leave to cool in the tin for 2–3 minutes, then turn out onto a
flameproof serving plate. Prick the cake all over with a skewer, then
sprinkle with the liqueur.

For the meringue topping, place the egg whites in a clean bowl and
whisk with a hand-held electric mixer until thick enough to hold
soft peaks. Gradually add the caster sugar, whisking vigorously
after each addition, then whisk in the coffee extract.

Spoon the meringue on top of the cake and spread into peaks and
swirls with a palette knife. Use a chef's blowtorch to brown the
meringue or place the cake under a hot grill for 2–3 minutes, or
until just browned but still soft inside. Cut into slices and serve.

Chocolate & Cherry Gateau

serves 8

oil or melted butter, for
greasing
150 g/5½ oz plain flour
2 tbsp cocoa powder
1 tbsp baking powder
175 g/6 oz unsalted
butter, softened
175 g/6 oz golden caster
sugar
3 eggs, beaten
1 tsp vanilla extract
2 tbsp milk
3 tbsp kirsch or
brandy (optional)
grated chocolate and fresh
whole cherries, to decorate

filling and topping
450 ml/16 fl oz double or
whipping cream
2 tbsp icing sugar
225 g/8 oz fresh dark red
cherries, stoned

Preheat the oven to 180°C/350°F/Gas Mark 4. Grease two 20-cm/8-inch sandwich cake tins and line the bases with baking paper.

Sift the flour, cocoa and baking powder into a large bowl and add the butter, caster sugar, eggs and vanilla extract. Beat well until the mixture is smooth, then stir in the milk.

Divide the mixture between the prepared tins and smooth level. Bake in the preheated oven for 25–30 minutes, or until risen and firm to the touch. Leave to cool in the tins for 2–3 minutes, then turn out and finish cooling on wire racks.

When the cakes are cold, sprinkle with the kirsch, if using. For the filling and topping, whip the cream with the icing sugar until thick, then spread about a third over the top of one of the cakes. Spread the cherries over the cream and place the second cake on top.

Spread the remaining cream over the top and sides of the cake and decorate with grated chocolate and fresh whole cherries.

Double Chocolate Mint Sponge

serves 8

oil or melted butter,
for greasing

150 g/5½ oz plain flour

2 tbsp cocoa powder

1 tbsp baking powder

175 g/6 oz unsalted butter,
softened

175 g/6 oz caster sugar

3 eggs, beaten

1 tbsp milk

40 g/1½ oz chocolate mint
sticks, chopped

140 g/5 oz chocolate spread,
plus extra to drizzle

chocolate mint sticks
to decorate

Preheat the oven to 180°C/350°F/Gas Mark 4. Grease two 20-cm/8-inch sandwich cake tins and line with baking paper.

Sift the flour, cocoa and baking powder into a bowl and beat in the butter, sugar and eggs, mixing until smooth. Stir in the milk and chocolate mint pieces.

Spread the mixture into the prepared tins. Bake in the preheated oven for 25–30 minutes, until risen and firm. Cool in the tin for 2 minutes, then turn out onto a wire rack to finish cooling.

Sandwich the cakes together with chocolate spread and decorate with chocolate mint sticks. Drizzle chocolate spread over the top.

Deep Chocolate Cheesecake

serves 6–8

oil or melted butter,
for greasing

115 g/4 oz digestive biscuits,
finely crushed

2 tsp cocoa powder

55 g/2 oz butter, melted

chocolate leaves, to decorate

filling

800 g/1 lb 12 oz mascarpone
cheese

200 g/7 oz icing sugar, sifted

juice of ½ orange

finely grated rind of 1 orange

175 g/6 oz plain chocolate,
melted

2 tbsp brandy

Grease a 20-cm/8-inch loose-based round cake tin.

Put the crushed biscuits, cocoa powder and melted butter into a large bowl and mix well. Press the biscuit mixture evenly over the base of the prepared tin.

For the filling, put the mascarpone cheese and icing sugar into a bowl and stir in the orange juice and rind. Add the melted chocolate and brandy and mix together until thoroughly combined. Spread the chocolate mixture evenly over the biscuit layer. Cover with clingfilm and chill for at least 4 hours.

Remove the cheesecake from the refrigerator, turn out onto a serving platter and decorate with chocolate leaves. Serve immediately.

Hot Chocolate Cheesecake

serves 8–10

oil or melted butter,
for greasing
150 g/5½ oz plain flour,
plus extra for dusting
2 tbsp cocoa powder
55 g/2 oz butter
2 tbsp golden caster sugar
25 g/1 oz ground almonds
1 egg yolk
icing sugar, for dusting
grated chocolate, to decorate

filling

2 eggs, separated
75 g/2¾ oz golden
caster sugar
350 g/12 oz cream cheese
4 tbsp ground almonds
150 ml/5 fl oz double cream
25 g/1 oz cocoa powder,
sifted
1 tsp vanilla extract

Grease a 20-cm/8-inch loose-based round cake tin.

Sift the flour and cocoa into a bowl and rub in the butter with your fingertips until the mixture resembles fine breadcrumbs. Stir in the sugar and ground almonds. Add the egg yolk and enough water to make a soft dough.

Roll out the pastry on a lightly floured work surface and use to line the prepared tin. Leave to chill for 30 minutes. Preheat the oven to 160°C/325°F/Gas Mark 3.

For the filling, put the egg yolks and sugar in a large bowl and whisk until thick and pale. Whisk in the cream cheese, ground almonds, cream, cocoa and vanilla extract until well combined.

Put the egg whites in a large bowl and whisk until stiff but not dry. Stir a little of the egg whites into the cheese mixture, then fold in the remainder. Pour into the pastry case.

Bake in the preheated oven for 1½ hours, until well risen and just firm to the touch. Carefully remove from the tin, dust with icing sugar and sprinkle with grated chocolate. Serve the cheesecake warm.

Chocolate Cake with Syrup

serves 12

oil or melted butter,
for greasing
225 g/8 oz plain chocolate,
broken into pieces
115 g/4 oz butter
1 tbsp strong black coffee
4 large eggs
2 egg yolks
115 g/4 oz caster sugar
40 g/1½ oz plain flour
2 tsp ground cinnamon
85 g/3 oz ground almonds
chocolate-covered coffee
beans, to decorate

syrup
300 ml/10 fl oz strong
black coffee
115 g/4 oz caster sugar
1 cinnamon stick

Preheat the oven to 190°C/375°F/Gas Mark 5. Grease a 20-cm/8-inch round deep cake tin and line with baking paper.

Place the chocolate, butter and coffee in a heatproof bowl and set over a saucepan of gently simmering water until melted. Stir to blend, then remove from the heat and leave to cool slightly.

Place the whole eggs, egg yolks and sugar in a separate bowl and whisk together until thick and pale. Sift the flour and cinnamon over the egg mixture. Add the almonds and the chocolate mixture and fold in carefully. Spoon the mixture into the prepared tin. Bake in the preheated oven for 35 minutes, or until the tip of a knife inserted into the centre comes out clean. Leave to cool slightly before turning out on to a serving plate.

For the syrup, place the coffee, sugar and cinnamon stick in a heavy-based saucepan and heat gently, stirring, until the sugar has dissolved. Increase the heat and boil for 5 minutes, or until reduced and thickened slightly. Keep warm. Pierce the surface of the cake with a cocktail stick, then drizzle over half the coffee syrup. Decorate with chocolate-covered coffee beans and serve, cut into wedges, with the remaining coffee syrup.

Cupcakes

Cupcakes

for perfect pick-me-ups

This edition published by Parragon Books Ltd in 2013
LOVE FOOD is an imprint of Parragon Books Ltd

Parragon Books Ltd
Chartist House
15–17 Trim Street
Bath BA1 1HA, UK
www.parragon.com/lovefood

ISBN 978-1-4723-0425-4

Printed in China

Notes for the Reader
This book uses both metric and imperial measurements. Follow the same units of
measurement throughout; do not mix metric and imperial. All spoon measurements are
level: teaspoons are assumed to be 5 ml, and tablespoons are assumed to be 15 ml. Unless
otherwise stated, milk is assumed to be full fat, eggs and individual vegetables are medium,
and pepper is freshly ground black pepper.

Garnishes, decorations and serving suggestions are all optional and not necessarily
included in the recipe ingredients or method. The times given are an approximate guide only.
Preparation times differ according to the techniques used by different people and the cooking
times may also vary from those given. Optional ingredients, variations or serving suggestions
have not been included in the time calculations.

Recipes using raw or very lightly cooked eggs should be avoided by infants, the elderly,
pregnant women, convalescents and anyone suffering from an illness. Pregnant and
breastfeeding women are advised to avoid eating peanuts and peanut products. Sufferers
from nut allergies should be aware that some of the ready-made ingredients used in the
recipes in this book may contain nuts. Always check the packaging before use.

Contents

Introduction

Who can resist a cupcake? These diminutive cakes are loved by all and are the perfect little treat to indulge in at any time. They are easy to make, fun, pretty and add that little touch of extravagance to any event, from a birthday to Christmas and even weddings.

This book is full of tempting ideas to treat yourself, family and friends and includes classic cupcakes through to more elaborate recipes to ensure you're never short of ideas for these irresistible and individual cakes.

Baking is a science as well as an art, so it is important to follow the recipes precisely. Before you start, read through the recipe and gather together all of the required ingredients and equipment. Specialist equipment is not necessary as most kitchens will have the essentials; these are measuring scales, mixing bowls, a wooden spoon, baking trays and bun tins. Buying the correct cases is also important as they help retain that characteristic cupcake shape but also help keep them fresh and moist. Fluted paper or foil baking cases are perfect but you can also now buy reusable, silicone cases that are brightly coloured and do the job just as well.

Follow the top tips on the opposite page to ensure perfect results and you'll soon realize there is no time like the present to dig out your apron, get baking and rediscover the joy of baking a batch of cupcake delights!

• Turn on the oven before you start in order to preheat it to the correct temperature while you're mixing.

• Use the baking times for each recipe as a guideline only. Temperatures vary widely from appliance to appliance. Being aware of this will ensure the best results every time.

• Always use eggs at room temperature. If you store eggs in the refrigerator, remove them about 30 minutes before use to allow them to come up to room temperature.

• Avoid over-mixing because this can cause a heavy texture – beat the mixture until just smooth.

• Bake the cupcakes immediately once mixed because the raising agents begin to act as soon as they're combined with liquid.

• Avoid opening the oven during cooking – this reduces the oven temperature and can cause the cupcakes to sink. Do however check just a few minutes before the end of the baking time to see how the cupcakes are progressing.

• Test for doneness – the cupcakes should be well risen and springy to the touch.

Everyday Cupcakes

Lemon Butterfly Cakes

makes 12

115 g/4 oz self-raising flour

½ tsp baking powder

115 g/4 oz butter, softened,
or soft margarine

115 g/4 oz caster sugar

2 eggs

finely grated rind of
½ lemon

2 tbsp milk

frosting

85 g/3 oz butter, softened

175 g/6 oz icing sugar

1 tbsp lemon juice

Preheat the oven to 190°C/375°F/Gas Mark 5. Put 12 paper baking cases in a bun tin or put 12 double-layer paper cases on a baking tray.

Sift the flour and baking powder into a large bowl, add the butter, sugar, eggs, lemon rind and milk and beat together until smooth. Spoon the mixture into the paper cases.

Bake in the preheated oven for 15–20 minutes, or until well risen and springy to the touch. Transfer to a wire rack to cool completely.

To make the frosting, place the butter in a bowl and beat until light and fluffy. Sift in the icing sugar, add the lemon juice and beat together until smooth and creamy. When the cupcakes are cold, cut the top off each cake then cut the top in half.

Spread or pipe a little of the lemon frosting over the cut surface of each cupcake, then gently press the 2 cut cake pieces into it at an angle to resemble butterfly wings.

Rose Petal Cupcakes

makes 12

115 g/4 oz butter, softened
115 g/4 oz caster sugar
2 eggs, lightly beaten
1 tbsp milk
few drops of essence of rose
oil
¼ tsp vanilla extract
175 g/6 oz self-raising flour
silver dragées,
to decorate

crystallized rose petals
12–24 rose petals
lightly beaten egg white, for
brushing
caster sugar, for sprinkling

frosting
85 g/3 oz butter, softened
175 g/6 oz icing sugar
pink or purple food colouring
(optional)

To make the crystallized rose petals, gently rinse the petals and dry well with kitchen paper. Using a pastry brush, paint both sides of a rose petal with egg white, then coat well with caster sugar. Place on a tray and repeat with the remaining petals. Cover the tray with foil and leave overnight.

Preheat the oven to 200°C/400°F/Gas Mark 6. Put 12 paper baking cases in a bun tin or put 12 double-layer paper cases on a baking tray.

Place the butter and sugar in a large bowl and beat together until light and fluffy, then gradually beat in the eggs. Stir in the milk, rose essence and vanilla extract, then fold in the flour. Spoon the mixture into the paper cases.

Bake in the preheated oven for 12–15 minutes, or until well risen and springy to the touch. Transfer to a wire rack to cool completely.

To make the frosting, place the butter in a large bowl and beat until light and fluffy. Sift in the icing sugar and mix well together. Add a few drops of pink or purple food colouring to match the rose petals, if liked.

When the cupcakes are cold, spread the frosting on top of each cake. Top with 1–2 crystallized rose petals and sprinkle with silver dragées.

Banoffee Cupcakes

makes 4

100 g/3½ oz butter, softened, plus extra for greasing

100 g/3½ oz soft light brown sugar

2 eggs, lightly beaten

100 g/3½ oz self-raising flour

1 small ripe banana, peeled and mashed

topping

150 ml/5 fl oz double cream

½ banana, peeled and sliced

2 tbsp dulce de leche (toffee sauce)

1 tbsp grated chocolate

Preheat the oven to 190°C/375°F/Gas Mark 5. Grease 4 x 200-ml/7-fl oz ovenproof teacups or dishes (such as ramekins) with butter.

Put the butter and sugar in a bowl and beat together until light and fluffy. Gradually beat in the eggs. Sift in the flour and, using a metal spoon, fold into the mixture with the mashed banana. Spoon the mixture into the cups or dishes.

Put the teacups or dishes on a baking sheet and bake in the preheated oven for 20–25 minutes, or until well risen and golden brown. Transfer to a wire rack to cool completely.

For the topping, whisk the cream in a bowl until softly peaking. Spoon the whipped cream on top of each cupcake then arrange 3–4 banana slices on top. Drizzle over the dulce de leche and sprinkle over the grated chocolate. Store the cupcakes in the refrigerator until ready to serve.

Chewy Flapjack Cupcakes

makes 8

55 g/2 oz butter, softened
55 g/2 oz golden caster sugar
1 large egg, lightly beaten
55 g/2 oz self-raising flour

topping
40 g/1½ oz soft tub margarine
40 g/1½ oz demerara sugar
1 tbsp golden syrup
55 g/2 oz rolled oats

Preheat the oven to 190°C/375°F/Gas Mark 5. Put 8 paper baking cases in a bun tin or put 8 double-layer paper cases on a baking tray.

To make the flapjack topping, place the margarine, demerara sugar and golden syrup in a small saucepan and heat gently until the margarine has melted. Stir in the oats. Set aside.

Put the butter and sugar in a bowl and beat together until light and fluffy. Gradually beat in the egg. Sift in the flour and, using a metal spoon, fold gently into the mixture. Spoon the mixture into the paper cases. Gently spoon the flapjack mixture over the top.

Bake in the preheated oven for 20 minutes, or until well risen and the topping is golden brown. Transfer to a wire rack to cool completely.

Iced Fairy Cakes

makes 16

115 g/4 oz butter, softened

115 g/4 oz caster sugar

2 eggs, lightly beaten

115 g/4 oz self-raising flour

sugar flowers, hundreds and thousands, glacé cherries and/ or chocolate strands, to decorate

icing

200 g/7 oz icing sugar

about 2 tbsp warm water

a few drops of food colouring (optional)

Preheat the oven to 190°C/375°F/Gas Mark 5. Put 16 paper baking cases in 2 x 12-hole bun tins or put 16 double-layer paper cases on a baking tray.

Place the butter and sugar in a large bowl and beat together until light and fluffy, then gradually beat in the eggs. Sift in the flour and fold into the mixture. Spoon the mixture into the paper cases.

Bake in the preheated oven for 15–20 minutes, or until well risen and springy to the touch. Transfer to a wire rack to cool completely.

To make the icing, sift the icing sugar into a bowl and stir in just enough warm water to mix to a smooth paste that is thick enough to coat the back of a wooden spoon. Stir in a few drops of food colouring, if using, then spread the icing over the fairy cakes and decorate, as liked.

Queen Cakes

makes 18

115 g/4 oz butter, softened, or soft margarine

115 g/4 oz caster sugar

2 large eggs, lightly beaten

4 tsp lemon juice

175 g/6 oz self-raising flour

115 g/4 oz currants

2–4 tbsp milk, if necessary

Preheat the oven to 190°C/375°F/Gas Mark 5. Put 18 paper baking cases in 2 x 12-hole bun tins or put 18 double-layer paper cases on a baking tray.

Place the butter and sugar in a large bowl and beat together until light and fluffy. Gradually beat in the eggs, then beat in the lemon juice with 1 tablespoon of the flour. Fold in the remaining flour and the currants. If necessary, add a little milk to give a soft dropping consistency. Spoon the mixture into the paper cases.

Bake in the preheated oven for 15–20 minutes, or until well risen and springy to the touch. Transfer to a wire rack to cool completely.

Rocky Road Cupcakes

makes 12

2 tbsp cocoa powder

2 tbsp hot water

115 g/4 oz butter, softened

115 g/4 oz caster sugar

2 eggs, lightly beaten

115 g/4 oz self-raising flour

topping

25 g/1 oz chopped mixed nuts

100 g/3½ oz milk chocolate, melted

115 g/4 oz mini marshmallows

40 g/1½ oz glacé cherries, chopped

Preheat the oven to 180°C/350°F/Gas Mark 4. Put 12 paper muffin cases in a muffin tin or put 12 double-layer paper cases on a baking tray.

Blend the cocoa powder and hot water together and set aside. Put the butter and sugar in a bowl and beat together until light and fluffy. Gradually beat in the eggs, then beat in the blended cocoa. Sift in the flour and, using a metal spoon, fold gently into the mixture. Spoon the mixture into the paper cases.

Bake in the preheated oven for 20 minutes, or until well risen and springy to the touch. Transfer to a wire rack to cool completely.

To make the topping, stir the nuts into the melted chocolate and spread a little of the mixture over the top of the cakes. Lightly stir the marshmallows and cherries into the remaining chocolate mixture and pile on top of the cupcakes. Leave to set.

Double Ginger Cupcakes

makes 12

175 g/6 oz plain flour

1 tbsp baking powder

2 tsp ground ginger

175 g/6 oz unsalted butter, softened

175 g/6 oz light muscovado sugar

3 eggs, beaten

25 g/1 oz crystallized stem ginger, finely chopped

diced crystallized ginger, to decorate

frosting

200 g/7 oz ricotta cheese

85 g/3 oz icing sugar, sifted

finely grated rind of 1 tangerine

Preheat the oven to 190°C/375°F/Gas Mark 5. Put 12 paper baking cases in a bun tin or put 12 double-layer paper cases on a baking tray.

Sift the flour, baking powder and ground ginger into a large bowl. Add the butter, muscovado sugar and eggs and beat well until smooth. Stir in the crystallized stem ginger.

Spoon the mixture into the paper cases. Bake in the preheated oven for 15–20 minutes, or until well risen and springy to the touch. Transfer to a wire rack to cool completely.

For the frosting, mix together the ricotta, icing sugar and tangerine rind until smooth. Spoon a little frosting onto each cupcake and spread over the surface to cover. Decorate with the diced crystallized ginger and leave to set.

Moist Walnut Cupcakes

makes 12

85 g/3 oz walnuts

55 g/2 oz butter, softened, cut into small pieces

100 g/3½ oz caster sugar

grated rind of ½ lemon

70 g/2½ oz self-raising flour

2 eggs

12 walnut halves, to decorate

frosting

55 g/2 oz butter, softened

85 g/3 oz icing sugar

grated rind of ½ lemon

1 tsp lemon juice

Preheat the oven to 190°C/375°F/Gas Mark 5. Put 12 paper baking cases in a bun tin or put 12 double-layer paper cases on a baking tray.

Place the walnuts in a food processor and pulse until finely ground. Be careful not to overgrind, as the nuts will turn to oil.

Add the butter, caster sugar, lemon rind, flour and eggs and blend until the mixture is evenly combined. Spoon the mixture into the paper cases.

Bake in the preheated oven for 20 minutes, or until well risen and springy to the touch. Transfer to a wire rack to cool completely.

To make the frosting, place the butter in a bowl and beat together until light and fluffy. Sift in the icing sugar, add the lemon rind and juice and mix well together. When the cupcakes are cold, spread the frosting on top of each cupcake and top with a walnut half to decorate.

Frosted Peanut Butter Cupcakes

makes 16

55 g/2 oz butter, softened, or soft margarine

225 g/8 oz soft light brown sugar

115 g/4 oz crunchy peanut butter

2 eggs, lightly beaten

1 tsp vanilla extract

225 g/8 oz plain flour

2 tsp baking powder

100 ml/3½ fl oz milk

frosting

200 g/7 oz full-fat soft cream cheese

25 g/1 oz butter, softened

225 g/8 oz icing sugar

Preheat the oven to 180°C/350°F/Gas Mark 4. Put 16 paper muffin cases in 2 x 12-hole muffin tins or put 16 double-layer paper cases on a baking tray.

Place the butter, sugar and peanut butter in a bowl and beat together for 1–2 minutes, or until well mixed. Gradually beat in the eggs, then add the vanilla extract. Sift in the flour and baking powder, then fold them into the mixture, alternating with the milk. Spoon the mixture into the paper cases.

Bake in the preheated oven for 25 minutes, or until well risen and springy to the touch. Transfer to a wire rack to cool completely.

To make the frosting, place the cream cheese and butter in a large bowl and beat together until smooth. Sift the icing sugar into the mixture, beat together until well mixed, then spread the frosting on top of each cupcake.

Chocolate Box

Jumbo Chocolate Chip Cupcakes

makes 8

100 g/3½ oz butter, softened, or soft margarine

100 g/3½ oz caster sugar

2 large eggs

100 g/3½ oz self-raising flour

100 g/3½ oz plain chocolate chips

Preheat the oven to 190°C/375°F/Gas Mark 5. Put 8 paper muffin cases in a muffin tin or put 8 double-layer paper cases on a baking tray.

Place the butter, sugar, eggs and flour in a large bowl and beat together until just smooth. Fold in the chocolate chips. Spoon the mixture into the paper cases.

Bake in the preheated oven for 20–25 minutes, or until well risen and springy to the touch. Transfer to a wire rack to cool completely.

Chocolate Cupcakes with Cream Cheese Frosting

makes 18

85 g/3 oz butter, softened, or soft margarine

100 g/3½ oz caster sugar

2 eggs, lightly beaten

2 tbsp milk

55 g/2 oz plain chocolate chips

225 g/8 oz self-raising flour

25 g/1 oz cocoa powder

chocolate curls, to decorate

frosting

225 g/8 oz white chocolate, broken into pieces

150 g/5½ oz low-fat cream cheese

Preheat the oven to 200°C/400°F/Gas Mark 6. Put 18 paper baking cases in 2 x 12-hole bun tins or put 18 double-layer paper cases on a baking tray. Place the butter and sugar in a large bowl and beat together until light and fluffy, then gradually beat in the eggs. Add the milk, then fold in the chocolate chips. Sift in the flour and cocoa powder, then fold into the mixture. Spoon the mixture into the paper cases.

Bake in the preheated oven for 20 minutes, or until well risen and springy to the touch. Transfer to a wire rack to cool completely.

To make the frosting, place the white chocolate in a small heatproof bowl, set the bowl over a saucepan of gently simmering water and heat until melted. Leave to cool slightly. Place the cream cheese in a separate bowl and beat until softened, then beat in the slightly cooled chocolate.

When the cupcakes are cold, spread a little of the frosting over the top of each cupcake, then leave to chill in the refrigerator for 1 hour before serving. Decorate with a few chocolate curls.

Mocha Cupcakes with Whipped Cream

makes 20

2 tbsp instant espresso coffee powder

85 g/3 oz butter

85 g/3 oz caster sugar

1 tbsp clear honey

200 ml/7 fl oz water

225 g/8 oz plain flour

2 tbsp cocoa powder

1 tsp bicarbonate of soda

3 tbsp milk

1 large egg, lightly beaten

cocoa powder, for dusting

topping

225 ml/8 fl oz whipping cream

Preheat the oven to 180°C/350°F/Gas Mark 4. Put 20 paper baking cases in 2 x 12-hole bun tins or put 20 double-layer paper cases on a baking tray.

Place the coffee powder, butter, sugar, honey and water in a saucepan and heat gently, stirring, until the sugar has dissolved. Bring to the boil, then reduce the heat and leave to simmer for 5 minutes. Pour into a large heatproof bowl and leave to cool.

When the mixture has cooled, sift in the flour and cocoa powder. Place the bicarbonate of soda and milk in a bowl and stir to dissolve, then add to the mixture with the egg and beat together until smooth. Spoon the mixture into the paper cases.

Bake in the preheated oven for 15–20 minutes, or until well risen and springy to the touch. Transfer to a wire rack to cool completely.

For the topping, place the cream in a bowl and whip until it holds its shape. Spoon heaped teaspoonfuls of cream on top of each cupcake, then dust lightly with sifted cocoa powder.

Warm Molten-centred Chocolate Cupcakes

makes 6

55 g/2 oz butter, softened, or
soft margarine
55 g/2 oz caster sugar
1 large egg
85 g/3 oz self-raising flour
1 tbsp cocoa powder
55 g/2 oz plain chocolate
icing sugar, for dusting

Preheat the oven to 190°C/375°F/Gas Mark 5. Put 6 paper baking cases in a bun tin or put 6 double-layer paper cases on a baking tray.

Place the butter, sugar, egg, flour and cocoa powder in a large bowl and beat together until just smooth. Spoon half of the mixture into the paper cases. Using a teaspoon, make an indentation in the centre of each cake. Break the chocolate into 6 even squares and place a piece in each indentation, then spoon the remaining cake mixture on top.

Bake in the preheated oven for 20 minutes, or until well risen and springy to the touch. Leave the cupcakes in the tin for 2–3 minutes before serving warm, dusted with sifted icing sugar.

Marbled Chocolate Cupcakes

makes 21

175 g/6 oz soft margarine

175 g/6 oz caster sugar

3 eggs

175 g/6 oz self-raising flour

2 tbsp milk

55 g/2 oz plain chocolate, melted

Preheat the oven to 180°C/350°F/Gas Mark 4. Put 21 paper baking cases in 2 x 12-hole bun tins or put 21 double-layer paper cases on a baking tray.

Place the margarine, sugar, eggs, flour and milk in a large bowl and beat together until just smooth.

Divide the mixture between 2 bowls. Add the melted chocolate to one and stir until mixed. Using a teaspoon, and alternating the chocolate mixture with the plain, put 4 half-teaspoons into each case.

Bake in the preheated oven for 20 minutes, or until well risen and springy to the touch. Transfer to a wire rack to cool completely.

Double Chocolate Cupcakes

makes 18

85 g/3 oz white chocolate
1 tbsp milk
115 g/4 oz self-raising flour
½ tsp baking powder
115 g/4 oz butter, softened
115 g/4 oz caster sugar
2 eggs
1 tsp vanilla extract
18 white chocolate buttons,
to decorate

topping
140 g/5 oz milk chocolate

Preheat the oven to 190°C/375°F/Gas Mark 5. Put 18 paper baking cases in 2 x 12-hole bun tins, or put 18 double-layer paper cases on a baking tray.

Break the white chocolate into a heatproof bowl and add the milk. Set the bowl over a saucepan of gently simmering water and heat until melted. Remove from the heat and stir gently until smooth.

Sift the flour and baking powder into a bowl. Add the butter, sugar, eggs and vanilla extract and, using an electric hand whisk, beat together until smooth. Fold in the melted white chocolate. Spoon the mixture into the paper cases.

Bake in the preheated oven for 20 minutes, or until well risen and springy to the touch. Transfer to a wire rack and leave to cool completely.

To make the topping, break the chocolate into a heatproof bowl and set the bowl over a saucepan of gently simmering water until melted. Cool for 5 minutes then spread over the top of the cupcakes. Decorate each cupcake with a chocolate button.

Chocolate & Orange Cupcakes

makes 16

115 g/4 oz butter, softened

115 g/4 oz golden caster sugar

finely grated rind and juice of ½ orange

2 eggs, lightly beaten

115 g/4 oz self-raising flour

25 g/1 oz plain chocolate, grated

thin strips candied orange peel, to decorate

topping

115 g/4 oz plain chocolate, broken into pieces

25 g/1 oz unsalted butter

1 tbsp golden syrup

Preheat the oven to 180°C/350°F/Gas Mark 4. Put 16 paper baking cases in 2 x 12-hole bun tins or put 16 double-layer paper cases on a baking tray.

Put the butter, sugar and orange rind in a bowl and beat together until light and fluffy. Gradually beat in the eggs. Sift in the flour and, using a metal spoon, fold gently into the mixture with the orange juice and grated chocolate. Spoon the mixture into the paper cases.

Bake the cupcakes in the preheated oven for 20 minutes, or until well risen and springy to the touch. Transfer to a wire rack to cool completely.

To make the topping, break the chocolate into a heatproof bowl and add the butter and syrup. Set the bowl over a saucepan of gently simmering water and heat until melted. Remove from the heat and stir until smooth. Cool until the topping is thick enough to spread. Spread over the cupcakes and decorate each cupcake with a few strips of candied orange peel. Leave to set.

Chocolate Fruit & Nut Crispy Cakes

makes 18

300 g/10½ oz plain chocolate, broken into pieces

150 g/5½ oz butter, cut into cubes

250 g/9 oz golden syrup

100 g/3½ oz Brazil nuts, roughly chopped

100 g/3½ oz ready-to-eat dried raisins

200 g/7 oz cornflakes

18 glacé cherries, to decorate

Put 18 paper baking cases in 2 x 12-hole bun tins or put 18 double-layer paper cases on a baking tray.

Place the chocolate, butter and golden syrup into a large saucepan and heat gently until the butter has melted and the ingredients are runny but not hot. Remove from the heat and stir until well mixed.

Add the chopped nuts and raisins to the pan and stir together until the fruit and nuts are covered in chocolate. Add the cornflakes and stir until combined.

Spoon the mixture evenly into the paper cases and top each with a glacé cherry. Leave to set in a cool place for 2–4 hours before serving.

Devil's Food Cake with Chocolate Frosting

makes 18

50 g/1¾ oz butter, softened, or soft margarine
115 g/4 oz soft dark brown sugar
2 large eggs
115 g/4 oz plain white flour
½ tsp bicarbonate of soda
25 g/1 oz cocoa powder
125 ml/4 fl oz soured cream

frosting
125 g/4½ oz plain chocolate, broken into pieces
2 tbsp caster sugar
150 ml/5 fl oz soured cream

chocolate sticks (optional)
100 g/3½ oz plain chocolate

Preheat the oven to 180°C/350°F/Gas Mark 4. Put 18 paper baking cases in 2 x 12-hole bun tins or put 18 double-layer paper cases on a baking tray.

Place the butter, sugar, eggs, flour, bicarbonate of soda and cocoa powder in a large bowl and beat together until just smooth. Fold in the soured cream. Spoon the mixture into the paper cases.

Bake in the preheated oven for 20 minutes, or until well risen and springy to the touch. Transfer to a wire rack to cool completely.

To make the frosting, place the chocolate in a heatproof bowl, set over a saucepan of gently simmering water and heat until melted. Leave to cool slightly, then whisk in the sugar and soured cream until combined. Spread the frosting over the tops of the cakes and chill in the refrigerator before serving.

Decorate with chocolate sticks made by shaving plain chocolate with a potato peeler, if liked.

Chocolate Butterfly Cakes

makes 12

25 g/1 oz plain chocolate, broken into pieces
125 g/4½ oz butter, softened
125 g/4½ oz caster sugar
150 g/5½ oz self-raising flour
2 large eggs
2 tbsp cocoa powder
icing sugar, for dusting

frosting
100 g/3½ oz butter, softened
225 g/8 oz icing sugar
grated rind of ½ lemon
1 tbsp lemon juice

Preheat the oven to 180°C/350°F/Gas Mark 4. Put 12 paper baking cases in a bun tin or put 12 double-layer paper cases on a baking tray.

Place the chocolate in a heatproof bowl, set the bowl over a saucepan of gently simmering water and heat until melted, then leave to cool slightly.

Place the butter, sugar, flour, eggs and cocoa powder in a large bowl and beat together until the mixture is just smooth. Beat in the melted chocolate. Spoon the mixture into the paper cases.

Bake in the preheated oven for 15 minutes, or until well risen and springy to the touch. Transfer to a wire rack to cool completely.

To make the frosting, place the butter in a bowl and beat until light and fluffy, then gradually sift in the icing sugar and beat to combine. Beat in the lemon rind, then gradually beat in the lemon juice. When the cupcakes are cold, cut the top off each cake, then cut the top in half. Spread or pipe a little of the frosting over the cut surface of each cupcake, then gently press the 2 cut cake pieces into it at an angle to resemble butterfly wings. Dust with sifted icing sugar.

Feeling Fruity

Warm Strawberry Cupcakes
Baked in a Teacup

makes 6

115 g/4 oz butter, softened,
plus extra for greasing

4 tbsp strawberry jam

115 g/4 oz caster sugar

2 eggs, lightly beaten

1 tsp vanilla extract

115 g/4 oz self-raising flour

6 whole strawberries,
to decorate

icing sugar, for dusting

Preheat the oven to 180°C/350°F/Gas Mark 4. Grease 6 x 200-ml/7-fl oz ovenproof teacups or dishes (such as ramekins). Spoon 2 teaspoons of the strawberry jam into the bottom of each teacup.

Place the butter and sugar in a large bowl and beat together until light and fluffy. Gradually add the eggs, beating well after each addition, then add the vanilla extract. Sift in the flour and fold into the mixture. Spoon the mixture into the teacups.

Stand the cups in a roasting tin, then pour in enough hot water to come one third up the sides of the teacups. Bake in the preheated oven for 40 minutes, or until well risen and springy to the touch, and a skewer, inserted in the centre, comes out clean. If overbrowning, cover the cupcakes with a sheet of foil. Leave the cupcakes to cool for 2–3 minutes, then carefully lift the cups from the tin and place them on saucers.

Top each cupcake with a strawberry, then dust them with sifted icing sugar. Serve warm.

Fresh Raspberry Cupcakes

makes 12

275 g/9¾ oz fresh raspberries
150 ml/5 fl oz sunflower oil
2 eggs
140 g/5 oz caster sugar
½ tsp vanilla extract
275 g/9¾ oz plain flour
¾ tsp bicarbonate of soda
12 fresh raspberries, small
mint leaves, to decorate

topping
150 ml/5 fl oz double cream

Preheat the oven to 180°C/350°F/Gas Mark 4. Put 12 paper baking cases in a bun tin or put 12 double-layer paper cases on a baking tray.

Place the raspberries in a large bowl and crush lightly with a fork.

Place the oil, eggs, sugar and vanilla extract in a large bowl and whisk together until well combined. Sift in the flour and bicarbonate of soda and fold into the mixture, then fold in the crushed raspberries. Spoon the mixture into the paper cases.

Bake in the preheated oven for 30 minutes, or until well risen and springy to the touch. Leave the cupcakes to cool in the tin for 10 minutes, then transfer to a wire rack to cool completely.

When ready to decorate, place the cream in a bowl and whip until soft peaks form. Spread the cream on top of the cupcakes, using a knife to smooth the cream. Top each cupcake with a raspberry and decorate with mint leaves.

Apple Streusel Cupcakes

makes 14

½ tsp bicarbonate of soda
280 g/10 oz jar Bramley apple sauce
55 g/2 oz butter, softened, or soft margarine
85 g/3 oz demerara sugar
1 large egg, lightly beaten
175 g/6 oz self-raising flour
½ tsp ground cinnamon
½ tsp freshly ground nutmeg

topping
50 g/1¾ oz plain white flour
50 g/1¾ oz demerara sugar
¼ tsp ground cinnamon
¼ tsp freshly grated nutmeg
35 g/1¼ oz butter, cut into small pieces

Preheat the oven to 180°C/350°F/Gas Mark 4. Put 14 paper baking cases in 2 x 12-hole bun tins or put 14 double-layer paper cases in a baking tray.

First, make the topping. Place the flour, sugar, cinnamon and nutmeg in a large bowl. Add the butter and rub it in with your fingertips until the mixture resembles fine breadcrumbs. Reserve until required.

To make the cupcakes, add the bicarbonate of soda to the jar of apple sauce and stir until dissolved. Place the butter and sugar in a large bowl and beat together until light and fluffy, then gradually beat in the egg. Sift in the flour, cinnamon and nutmeg and fold into the mixture, alternating with the apple sauce. Spoon the mixture into the paper cases. Scatter the reserved topping over each cupcake to cover the tops and press down gently.

Bake in the preheated oven for 20 minutes, or until well risen and springy to the touch. Leave the cakes for 2–3 minutes in the tins before serving warm, or transfer to a wire rack to cool completely.

Lemon Meringue Cupcakes

makes 4

100 g/3½ oz butter, softened,
plus extra for greasing

100 g/3½ oz caster sugar

finely grated rind and juice of
½ lemon

1 large egg, lightly beaten

100 g/3½ oz self-raising flour,
sifted

2 tbsp lemon curd

meringue
2 egg whites

100 g/3½ oz caster sugar

Preheat the oven to 190°C/375°F/Gas Mark 5. Grease 4 x 200-ml/
7-fl oz ramekins with butter.

Put the butter, sugar and lemon rind into a mixing bowl and beat
together until light and fluffy. Gradually beat in the egg. Sift in
the flour and, using a metal spoon, fold into the mixture with the
lemon juice. Spoon the mixture into the ramekins.

Put the ramekins on a baking tray and bake in the preheated oven
for 15 minutes, or until well risen and springy to the touch.

While the cupcakes are baking, make the meringue. Put the egg
whites in a clean grease-free bowl and, using a hand-held electric
mixer, mix until stiff. Gradually whisk in the sugar to form a stiff
and glossy meringue.

When the cupcakes are cooked, remove from the oven. Spread the
lemon curd over the hot cupcakes, then swirl over the meringue.
Return the cupcakes to the oven for 4–5 minutes, until the
meringue is golden. Serve immediately.

Spiced Plum Cupcakes

makes 4

55 g/2 oz butter, softened,
plus extra for greasing

55 g/2 oz caster sugar

1 large egg, lightly beaten

55 g/2 oz plain wholemeal
flour

½ tsp baking powder

1 tsp ground mixed spice

25 g/1 oz blanched hazelnuts,
coarsely ground

2 small plums, halved, stoned
and sliced

Preheat the oven to 180°C/350°F/Gas Mark 4. Grease 4 x 150-ml/5-fl oz ramekins with butter.

Put the butter and sugar in a bowl and beat together until light and fluffy. Gradually beat in the egg. Sift in the flour, baking powder and mixed spice (tipping any bran left in the sieve into the bowl) and, using a metal spoon, fold into the mixture with the ground hazelnuts. Spoon the mixture into the ramekins. Arrange the sliced plums on top of the mixture.

Put the ramekins on a baking sheet and bake in the preheated oven for 25 minutes, or until well risen and firm to the touch.

Tropical Pineapple Cupcakes

makes 12

2 slices canned pineapple in natural juice

85 g/3 oz butter, softened, or soft margarine

85 g/3 oz caster sugar

1 large egg, lightly beaten

85 g/3 oz self-raising flour

frosting

25 g/1 oz butter, softened

100 g/3½ oz soft cream cheese

grated rind of 1 lemon or lime

100 g/3½ oz icing sugar

1 tsp lemon or lime juice

Preheat the oven to 180°C/350°F/Gas Mark 4. Put 12 paper baking cases in a bun tin or put 12 double-layer paper cases on a baking tray.

Drain the pineapple, reserving the juice. Finely chop the pineapple slices. Place the butter and sugar in a large bowl and beat together until light and fluffy, then gradually beat in the egg. Add the flour and fold into the mixture. Fold in the chopped pineapple and 1 tablespoon of the reserved pineapple juice. Spoon the mixture into the paper cases.

Bake in the preheated oven for 20 minutes, or until well risen and springy to the touch. Transfer to a wire rack to cool completely.

To make the frosting, place the butter and cream cheese in a large bowl and beat together until smooth, then add the lemon rind.

Sift the icing sugar into the mixture and beat together until well mixed. Gradually beat in the lemon juice, adding enough to form a spreading consistency.

When the cupcakes are cold, spread the frosting on top of each cake, or fill a piping bag fitted with a large star nozzle and pipe the frosting on top.

Coconut Cherry Cupcakes

makes 12

115 g/4 oz butter, softened, or soft margarine

115 g/4 oz caster sugar

2 tbsp milk

2 eggs, lightly beaten

85 g/3 oz self-raising flour

½ tsp baking powder

85 g/3 oz desiccated coconut

115 g/4 oz glacé cherries, quartered

12 whole glacé, maraschino or fresh cherries, to decorate

frosting

55 g/2 oz butter, softened

115 g/4 oz icing sugar

1 tbsp milk

Preheat the oven to 180°C/350°F/Gas Mark 4. Put 12 paper baking cases in a bun tin or put 12 double-layer paper cases on a baking tray.

Place the butter and sugar in a large bowl and beat together until light and fluffy. Stir in the milk and then gradually beat in the eggs. Sift in the flour and baking powder and fold them in with the coconut. Gently fold in most of the quartered cherries.

Spoon the mixture into the paper cases and scatter the remaining quartered cherries evenly on top.

Bake in the preheated oven for 20–25 minutes, or until well risen and springy to the touch. Transfer to a wire rack to cool completely.

To make the buttercream frosting, put the butter in a bowl and beat until light and fluffy. Sift in the icing sugar and beat together until well mixed, gradually beating in the milk.

When the cupcakes are cold, place the frosting in a piping bag fitted with a large star nozzle and pipe the frosting on top of each cupcake, then add a cherry to decorate.

Pistachio Cupcakes with Tangy Lime Frosting

makes 16

85 g/3 oz unsalted pistachio nuts

115 g/4oz butter, softened

140 g/5 oz golden caster sugar

140 g/5 oz self-raising flour

2 eggs, lightly beaten

4 tbsp Greek-style yoghurt

1 tbsp chopped pistachio nuts

frosting

115 g/4 oz butter, softened

2 tbsp lime juice cordial

few drops green food colouring (optional)

200 g/7 oz icing sugar

Preheat the oven to 180°C/350°F/Gas Mark 4. Put 16 paper baking cases in 2 x 12-hole bun tins or put 16 double-layer paper cases on a baking tray.

Put the pistachio nuts in a food processor or blender and process for a few seconds until finely ground. Add the butter, sugar, flour, eggs and yoghurt and then process until evenly mixed. Spoon the mixture into the paper cases.

Bake the cupcakes in the preheated oven for 20–25 minutes, or until well risen and springy to the touch. Transfer to a wire rack and leave to cool completely.

To make the frosting, put the butter, lime cordial and food colouring (if using) in a bowl and beat until light and fluffy. Sift in the icing sugar and beat until smooth. Swirl the frosting over each cupcake and sprinkle with the chopped pistachio nuts.

Banana & Pecan Cupcakes

makes 24

225 g/8 oz plain flour

1¼ tsp baking powder

¼ tsp bicarbonate of soda

2 ripe bananas

115 g/4 oz butter, softened, or soft margarine

115 g/4 oz caster sugar

⅓ tsp vanilla extract

2 eggs, lightly beaten

4 tbsp soured cream

55 g/2 oz pecan nuts, roughly chopped

25 g/1 oz pecan nuts, finely chopped, to decorate

frosting

115 g/4 oz butter, softened

115 g/4 oz icing sugar

Preheat the oven to 190°C/375°F/Gas Mark 5. Put 24 paper baking cases in 2 x 12-hole bun tins or put 24 double-layer paper cases on a baking tray.

Sift together the flour, baking powder and bicarbonate of soda. Place the bananas in a separate bowl and mash with a fork.

Place the butter, sugar and vanilla extract in a large bowl and beat together until light and fluffy, then gradually beat in the eggs. Stir in the mashed bananas and soured cream. Fold in the flour mixture and chopped nuts. Spoon the mixture into the paper cases.

Bake in the preheated oven for 20 minutes, or until well risen and springy to the touch. Transfer to a wire rack to cool completely.

To make the frosting, place the butter in a bowl and beat until light and fluffy. Sift in the icing sugar and mix together well. Spread the frosting on top of each cupcake and sprinkle with the finely chopped pecan nuts before serving.

Carrot & Orange Cupcakes

makes 12

115 g/4 oz butter, softened,
or soft margarine

115 g/4 oz soft light brown
sugar

finely grated rind and juice of
1 small orange

2 large eggs, lightly beaten

175 g/6 oz carrots, grated

25 g/1 oz walnut pieces,
roughly chopped

125 g/4½ oz plain flour

1 tsp ground mixed spice

1½ tsp baking powder

frosting

280 g/10 oz mascarpone
cheese

4 tbsp icing sugar

grated rind of 1 large orange

Preheat the oven to 180°C/350°F/Gas Mark 4. Put 12 paper muffin cases in a muffin tin or put 12 double-layer paper cases on a baking tray.

Place the butter, sugar and orange rind in a bowl and beat together until light and fluffy, then gradually beat in the eggs. Squeeze any excess liquid from the carrots and add to the mixture with the walnuts and orange juice. Stir until well mixed. Sift in the flour, mixed spice and baking powder and fold in. Spoon the mixture into the paper cases.

Bake in the preheated oven for 25 minutes, or until well risen and springy to the touch. Transfer to a wire rack to cool completely.

To make the frosting, place the mascarpone cheese, icing sugar and orange rind in a large bowl and beat together until they are well mixed.

When the cupcakes are cold, spread the frosting on top of each cupcake, swirling it with a round-bladed knife.

Festive Fancies

Birthday Party Cupcakes

makes 24

225 g/8 oz butter, softened, or soft margarine

225 g/8 oz caster sugar

4 eggs

225 g/8 oz self-raising flour

a variety of sweets and chocolates, sugar-coated chocolates, dried fruits, edible sugar flower shapes, cake decorating sprinkles, sugar strands and silver or gold dragées

various tubes of coloured writing icing

candles and candle holders (optional), to decorate

frosting

175 g/6 oz butter, softened

350 g/12 oz icing sugar

Preheat the oven to 180°C/350°F/Gas Mark 4. Put 24 paper baking cases in 2 x 12-hole bun tins or put 24 double-layer paper cases on a baking tray.

Place the butter, sugar, eggs and flour in a large bowl and beat together until just smooth. Spoon the mixture into the paper cases.

Bake in the preheated oven for 15–20 minutes, or until well risen and springy to the touch. Transfer to a wire rack to cool completely.

To make the frosting, place the butter in a bowl and beat until light and fluffy. Sift in the icing sugar and beat together until smooth and creamy. When the cupcakes are cold, spread the frosting on top of each cupcake, then decorate as you like and place a candle in the top of each, if using.

Valentine Heart Cupcakes

makes 6

85 g/3 oz butter, softened, or soft margarine

85 g/3 oz caster sugar

½ tsp vanilla extract

2 eggs, lightly beaten

70 g/2½ oz plain flour

1 tbsp cocoa powder

1 tsp baking powder

6 chocolate flowers, to decorate

marzipan hearts

icing sugar, for dusting

35 g/1¼ oz marzipan

red food colouring (liquid or paste)

topping

55 g/2 oz butter, softened

115 g/4 oz icing sugar

25 g/1 oz plain chocolate, melted

To make the hearts, line a baking sheet with baking paper and lightly dust with icing sugar. Knead the marzipan until pliable, then add a few drops of red colouring and knead until evenly coloured. Roll out the marzipan to a thickness of 5 mm/¼ inch on a surface dusted with icing sugar. Cut out 6 hearts with a small heart-shaped cutter and place on the sheet. Leave for 3–4 hours.

To make the cupcakes, preheat the oven to 180°C/350°F/ Gas Mark 4. Put 6 paper baking cases in a bun tin or put 6 double-layer paper cases on a baking tray.

Place the butter, sugar and vanilla extract in a large bowl and beat together until light and fluffy, then gradually beat in the eggs. Sift in the flour, cocoa powder and baking powder and fold into the mixture. Spoon the mixture into the paper cases.

Bake in the preheated oven for 20–25 minutes, or until well risen and springy to the touch. Transfer to a wire rack to cool completely.

To make the topping, place the butter in a bowl and beat until light and fluffy. Sift in the icing sugar and beat until smooth. Add the melted chocolate and beat until mixed. Spread the icing on top of each cupcake and decorate with a chocolate flower and a marzipan heart.

Easter Cupcakes

makes 12

115 g/4 oz butter, softened,
or soft margarine
115 g/4 oz caster sugar
2 eggs, lightly beaten
85 g/3 oz self-raising flour
25 g/1 oz cocoa powder
2 x 130-g/4¾-oz packets mini
sugar-coated chocolate eggs,
to decorate

frosting
85 g/3 oz butter, softened
175 g/6 oz icing sugar
1 tbsp milk
2–3 drops vanilla extract

Preheat the oven to 180°C/350°F/Gas Mark 4. Put 12 paper baking cases in a bun tin or put 12 double-layer paper cases on a baking tray.

Place the butter and sugar in a large bowl and beat together until light and fluffy, then gradually beat in the eggs. Sift in the flour and cocoa powder and fold into the mixture. Spoon the mixture into the paper cases.

Bake in the preheated oven for 15–20 minutes, or until well risen and springy to the touch. Transfer to a wire rack to cool completely.

To make the buttercream frosting, place the butter in a bowl and beat until light and fluffy. Sift in the icing sugar and beat together until well mixed, adding the milk and vanilla extract.

When the cupcakes are cold, place the frosting in a piping bag, fitted with a large star nozzle and pipe a circle around the edge of each cupcake to form a nest. Place chocolate eggs in the centre of each nest to decorate.

Baby Shower Cupcakes with Sugared Almonds

makes 24

400 g/14 oz butter, softened

400 g/14 oz caster sugar

finely grated rind of 2 lemons

8 eggs, lightly beaten

400 g/14 oz self-raising flour

24 sugared almonds, to decorate

icing

350 g/12 oz icing sugar

6–8 tsp hot water

red or blue food colouring (liquid or paste)

Preheat the oven to 180°C/350°F/Gas Mark 4. Put 24 paper baking cases in 2 x 12-hole bun tins or put 24 double-layer paper cases on a baking tray.

Place the butter, sugar and lemon rind in a large bowl and beat together until light and fluffy, then gradually beat in the eggs. Sift in the flour and fold into the mixture. Spoon the mixture into the paper cases.

Bake in the preheated oven for 20–25 minutes, or until well risen and springy to the touch. Transfer to a wire rack to cool completely.

When the cakes are cold, make the icing. Sift the icing sugar into a bowl, add the hot water and stir until smooth and thick enough to coat the back of a wooden spoon. Dip a skewer into the red or blue food colouring and stir it into the icing until it is evenly coloured pink or pale blue. Spoon the icing on top of each cupcake. Top each cupcake with a sugared almond and leave to set for about 30 minutes.

Spring-time Cupcakes

makes 24

150 g/5½ oz butter, softened, or soft margarine

150 g/5½ oz caster sugar

1 tsp vanilla extract

2 large eggs, lightly beaten

140 g/5 oz self-raising flour

40 g/1½ oz cornflour

coloured sugar strands, to decorate

icing

115 g/4 oz ready-to-roll fondant icing

yellow and green food colourings

300 g/10½ oz icing sugar

about 3 tbsp cold water

Preheat the oven to 190°C/375°F/Gas Mark 5. Put 24 paper baking cases in 2 x 12-hole bun tins or put 24 double-layer paper cases on a baking tray. Place the butter and sugar in a large bowl and beat together until light and fluffy, then beat in the vanilla extract. Gradually beat in the eggs. Sift in the flour and cornflour and fold into the mixture. Spoon the mixture into the paper cases.

Bake in the preheated oven for 12–15 minutes, or until well risen and springy to the touch. Transfer to a wire rack to cool completely.

To make the icing, divide the fondant in half and colour one half pale yellow. Roll out both halves, then use the sides of a round pastry cutter to cut out white and yellow petal shapes. Set aside.

Sift the icing sugar into a bowl and mix with the water until smooth. Place half of the icing in a small piping bag fitted with a small plain nozzle. Divide the remaining icing in half and colour one portion yellow and the other green.

Cover 12 cupcakes with yellow icing and 12 with green icing. Arrange white petals on top of the yellow icing to form flowers. Pipe a little blob of white icing into the centre of each flower, then sprinkle a few coloured sugar strands on top of the white icing to form the centre of the flower. Arrange the yellow petals on the green icing and decorate in the same way. Leave to set.

Halloween Cupcakes

makes 12

115 g/4 oz butter, softened,
or soft margarine
115 g/4 oz caster sugar
2 eggs
115 g/4 oz self-raising flour

icing
200 g/7 oz orange ready-to-
roll coloured fondant icing
icing sugar, for dusting
55 g/2 oz black ready-to-roll
coloured fondant icing
black writing icing
white writing icing

Preheat the oven to 180°C/350°F/Gas Mark 4. Put 12 paper baking cases in a bun tin or put 12 double-layer paper cases on a baking tray.

Place the butter, sugar, eggs and flour in a large bowl and beat together until smooth. Spoon the mixture into the paper cases.

Bake in the preheated oven for 15–20 minutes, or until well risen and springy to the touch. Transfer to a wire rack to cool completely.

When the cupcakes are cold, knead the orange icing until pliable, then roll out on a surface dusted with icing sugar. Rub icing sugar into the icing to prevent it from spotting.

Cut out 12 circles with a 5.5-cm/2¼-inch round cutter, re-rolling the icing as necessary. Place a circle on top of each cupcake.

Roll out the black icing on a surface dusted with icing sugar. Rub icing sugar into the icing to prevent spotting. Cut out 12 circles with a 3-cm/1¼-inch round cutter and place them in the centre of the cupcake. Using black writing icing, pipe 8 legs onto each spider and draw eyes and a mouth with white writing icing. Leave to set.

Christmas Cupcakes

makes 12

125 g/4½ oz butter, softened
200 g/7 oz caster sugar
4–6 drops almond extract
4 eggs, lightly beaten
150 g/5½ oz self-raising flour
175 g/6 oz ground almonds

topping

450 g/1 lb white ready-to-roll fondant icing
icing sugar, for dusting
55 g/2 oz green ready-to-roll coloured fondant icing
25 g/1 oz red ready-to-roll coloured fondant icing

Preheat the oven to 180°C/350°F/Gas Mark 4. Put 12 paper baking cases in a bun tin or put 12 double-layer paper cases on a baking tray.

Place the butter, sugar and almond extract in a large bowl and beat together until light and fluffy, then gradually beat in the eggs. Sift in the flour and fold into the mixture, then fold in the ground almonds. Spoon the mixture into the paper cases.

Bake in the preheated oven for 20 minutes, or until well risen and springy to the touch. Transfer to a wire rack to cool completely.

When the cupcakes are cold, knead the white icing until pliable, then roll out on a surface lightly dusted with icing sugar. Cut out 12 circles with a 7-cm/2¾-inch plain round cutter, re-rolling the icing as necessary. Place a circle on top of each cupcake.

Roll out the green icing on a surface lightly dusted with icing sugar. Rub icing sugar into the icing to prevent it from spotting. Cut out 24 leaves with a holly leaf-shaped cutter, re-rolling the icing as necessary. Brush each leaf with a little cooled boiled water and place 2 leaves on top of each cupcake. Roll the red icing between the palms of your hands to form 36 berries and place 3 in the centre of the leaves on each cupcake, to decorate.

Festive Cupcakes

makes 14

115 g/4 oz mixed dried fruit
1 tsp finely grated orange rind
2 tbsp brandy or orange juice
85 g/3 oz butter, softened
85 g/3 oz light soft brown sugar
1 large egg, lightly beaten
115 g/4 oz self-raising flour
1 tsp ground mixed spice
1 tbsp silver dragées, to decorate

icing

85 g/3 oz icing sugar
2 tbsp orange juice

Put the mixed fruit, orange rind and brandy or orange juice in a small bowl and cover and leave to soak for 1 hour.

Preheat the oven to 190°C/375°F/Gas Mark 5. Put 14 paper baking cases in 2 x 12-hole bun tins or put 14 double-layer paper cases on a baking tray.

Put the butter and sugar in a mixing bowl and beat together until light and fluffy. Gradually beat in the egg. Sift in the flour and mixed spice and, using a metal spoon, fold them into the mixture followed by the soaked fruit. Spoon the mixture into the paper cases.

Bake the cupcakes in the preheated oven for 15–20 minutes, or until well risen and springy to the touch. Transfer to a cooling rack and leave to cool completely.

To make the icing, sift the icing sugar into a bowl and gradually mix in enough orange juice until the mixture is smooth and thick enough to coat the back of a wooden spoon. Using a teaspoon, drizzle the icing in a ziz-zag pattern over the cupcakes. Decorate with the silver dragées. Leave to set.

Wedding Day Fancy Favours

makes 12

115 g/4 oz butter, softened
100 g/3½ oz caster sugar
2 eggs, lightly beaten
140 g/5 oz self-raising flour, sifted
½ tsp vanilla extract
1–2 tbsp milk

topping
icing sugar, for dusting
225 g/8oz white ready-to-roll fondant icing
3 tbsp runny honey, warmed
2–3 drops pink food colouring
tube of green writing icing

Preheat the oven to 200°C/400°F/Gas Mark 6. Put 12 paper baking cases in a muffin tin or put 12 double-layer paper cases on a baking tray.

Place the butter and caster sugar into a mixing bowl and beat together for 1–2 minutes, until pale and creamy. Gradually add the eggs and continue beating. Fold in the flour using a metal spoon. Stir in the vanilla extract and milk.

Spoon the mixture into the paper cases. Bake in the preheated oven for 15-20 minutes, or until well risen and springy to the touch. Remove from the oven and leave to cool for 5 minutes in the tin, then move the cupcakes to a wire rack to cool completely.

Dust the work surface with some icing sugar. Roll out all but one eighth of the fondant icing to 20 x 28 cm/8 x 11 inches. Use a biscuit cutter to stamp out 12 rounds. Brush the cake tops with some honey and stick on the rounds.

For the rosebuds, knead the remaining icing with the food colouring. Rub icing sugar into the icing to prevent it from spotting. Roll out 12 strips of icing to 1 x 6 cm/½ x 2½ inch. Roll up from one end and stick onto the cake with a dab of honey. Draw on a stalk and leaves with the writing icing. Leave to set.

Gold & Silver Anniversary Cupcakes

makes 24

225 g/8 oz butter, softened
225 g/8 oz caster sugar
1 tsp vanilla extract
4 large eggs, lightly beaten
225 g/8 oz self-raising flour
5 tbsp milk
25 g/1 oz silver or gold dragées, to decorate

frosting
175 g/6 oz butter
350 g/12 oz icing sugar

Preheat the oven to 180°C/350°F/Gas Mark 4. Put 24 paper baking cases in 2 x 12-hole bun tins or put 24 double-layer paper cases on a baking tray.

Place the butter, sugar and vanilla extract in a large bowl and beat together until light and fluffy, then gradually beat in the eggs. Sift in the flour and fold into the mixture with the milk. Spoon the mixture into the paper cases.

Bake in the preheated oven for 15–20 minutes, or until well risen and springy to the touch. Transfer to a wire rack to cool completely.

To make the frosting, place the butter in a large bowl and beat until light and fluffy. Sift in the icing sugar and beat together until well mixed. Place the frosting in a piping bag fitted with a medium star-shaped nozzle.

When the cupcakes are cold, pipe circles of frosting on top of each cake to cover the tops and sprinkle over the silver or gold dragées.

Macaroons

Macaroons

for perfect bite-size treats

This edition published by Parragon Books Ltd in 2013
LOVE FOOD is an imprint of Parragon Books Ltd

Parragon Books Ltd
Chartist House
15–17 Trim Street
Bath BA1 1HA, UK
www.parragon.com/lovefood

ISBN 978-1-4723-0422-3

Printed in China

Photography by Clive Streeter
Recipes and home economy by Angela Drake

Notes for the Reader
This book uses both metric and imperial measurements. Follow the same units of
measurement throughout; do not mix metric and imperial. All spoon measurements are
level: teaspoons are assumed to be 5 ml, and tablespoons are assumed to be 15 ml. Unless
otherwise stated, milk is assumed to be full fat, eggs and individual vegetables are medium,
and pepper is freshly ground black pepper.

Garnishes, decorations and serving suggestions are all optional and not necessarily
included in the recipe ingredients or method. The times given are an approximate guide only.
Preparation times differ according to the techniques used by different people and the cooking
times may also vary from those given. Optional ingredients, variations or serving suggestions
have not been included in the time calculations.

Recipes using raw or very lightly cooked eggs should be avoided by infants, the elderly,
pregnant women, convalescents and anyone suffering from an illness. Pregnant and
breastfeeding women are advised to avoid eating peanuts and peanut products. Sufferers
from nut allergies should be aware that some of the ready-made ingredients used in the
recipes in this book may contain nuts. Always check the packaging before use.

Contents

Introduction

French *macarons* or macaroons are small almond meringues sandwiched together with a flavoured filling to make delightful bite-sized sweet treats. Made from egg whites, ground almonds, and caster and icing sugars, they are characterized by their smooth domed tops, frilly edged bases and wonderfully soft and slightly chewy centres. Popular in French patisseries, where a dazzling array of colours and flavours can be found, macaroons are the perfect after-dinner treat, sweet gift, teatime fancy or wedding favour.

As simple as they look, macaroons can be a little tricky to make – indeed pastry chefs can spend years perfecting the art of macaroons. But don't let that put you off because this book has everything you need to know for successful macaroon making – from a guide to the essential equipment and ingredients you will need, to clear and detailed step-by-step instructions for the basic method used to make all the macaroons in the book.

Once you've mastered the basic technique, you can try any one of the 30 deliciously different macaroons in this book. From classic flavours, such as vanilla, chocolate and pistachio, to more unusual combinations, such as sesame and lime or even peanut butter and jam, you'll be spoilt for choice.

So what are you waiting for? You may not quite achieve the high standards of a French pastry chef with your first few batches, but follow the top tips on the opposite and following pages and you'll soon find that the art of making macaroons is a pleasurable pastime with the most fabulous results!

- If your piping skills are not too good, mark circles on the baking paper by dipping a small cutter or the end of a large piping nozzle into icing sugar and tapping it onto the paper. It's not a problem if the circles vary in size – just match up the macaroons according to size when pairing them together.

- Use the oven temperature stated in the recipes as a guide – once you have made a couple of batches of macaroons you may find that the temperature of your oven needs reducing or increasing a little to achieve the best results. Use an oven thermometer if you have one. Fan ovens cook more quickly than conventional ovens so reduce the temperature by 10–20°C/50–68°F. You may also find that they cook the macaroons a little quicker – usually in about 9–10 minutes. On the other hand, gas ovens produce a more uneven, moist heat so try leaving the oven door slightly ajar to allow any steam to escape and rotate the sheet after 5–6 minutes.

- If you find that the bases of the macaroons are browning too quickly, place the baking sheet on a second baking sheet to diffuse the heat. If the tops of the macaroons crack, the oven temperature is too high.

- If the macaroon shells stick to the baking paper, try spraying a little water between the paper and baking sheet to create a little steam, which will help to release them.

- Unfilled macaroons will keep for 3–4 days in an airtight container or freeze for up to 1 month. Filled macaroons will keep in the fridge for 2–3 days, depending on the type of filling. They are best eaten at room temperature a few hours after filling.

10 Steps to Macaroon Perfection

Refer to this simple step-by-step guide when making any of the macaroon recipes in the book.

STEP 1: Place the ground almonds and icing sugar in a food processor and process for about 15 seconds, until the mixture is fine and powdery. Sift the mixture into a bowl through a large sieve. Discard any fine bits of almond left in the sieve.

STEP 2: Whisk the egg whites until holding soft peaks. Gradually whisk in the caster sugar, about 1 tablespoon at a time. Whisk well after each addition to make a firm and glossy meringue. The meringue should look like shaving cream and hold stiff peaks when the whisk is lifted from the bowl.

STEP 3: Add one third of the almond mixture to the meringue. Using a spatula, fold the dry mixture into the meringue. Use a circular folding action by running the spatula around the bowl and under the meringue then folding and cutting through the mixture.

STEP 4: Once all the dry mixture has been folded into the meringue, add the second third of the almond mixture, repeating the folding and cutting action. As more dry ingredients are folded into the meringue it will become firmer.

STEP 5: Add the final third of the almond mixture and repeat the folding and cutting action. Once all the dry ingredients have been incorporated the mixture will be quite firm so continue mixing until the consistency of the mixture loosens. The final batter should be smooth and glossy and a thick ribbon of batter should fall slowly from the spatula, leaving a trail for about 30 seconds before disappearing.

Important: Under-mixing the macaroon mixture will result in a batter that is too firm and the piped macaroons will have peaks. Over-mixing will result in a runny batter that will not hold its shape when piped. Check the batter every few turns of the spatula to avoid over-mixing.

STEP 6: Line two baking sheets with baking paper. Pour the mixture into a large piping bag fitted with a 1-cm/½-inch nozzle. Pipe 3-cm/1¼-inch rounds onto the prepared baking sheets. Make sure the rounds are well spaced. For large macaroons pipe 7-cm/2¾-inch rounds and for mini macaroons pipe 2-cm/¾-inch rounds.

STEP 7: Tap the underside of the baking sheets firmly with the palm of your hand or tap onto a work surface to remove any air bubbles and settle any small peaks and bumps. This action also helps the frilly foot (or *pied*) to form during baking. Any peaks still remaining can be flattened by dabbing gently with a wetted fingertip.

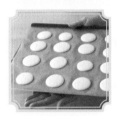

STEP 8: Leave the macaroons to stand at room temperature for 30 minutes to allow the surface of each macaroon to dry and form a slight crust. You should be able to gently touch the surface without any mixture sticking to your finger.

STEP 9: Bake the macaroons, one baking sheet at a time. Check after 5–6 minutes – if they are overbrowning, reduce the oven temperature slightly. Cooking time will take 10–15 minutes, depending on your oven, so check again after 10 minutes. The macaroons are ready when they have a crisp shell and the frilly foot at the base does not wobble when the shells are gently lifted from the paper. If the bases are still soft and sticky, return the trays to the oven for a further few minutes, leaving the door ajar.

STEP 10: Leave the macaroons to cool on the baking sheets for 10 minutes. Carefully peel them away from the paper. Leave to cool completely on a wire rack.

Essential Equipment

Scales
Accurate measuring is one of the major keys to success when making macaroons. Always follow the same units of measurement – do not mix metric and imperial.

Food processor
To achieve a really finely ground almond and icing sugar mixture you will need a food processor with a sharp blade. A large blender will work just as well. A coffee or spice grinder will also be useful for finely grinding nuts and seeds to flavour the macaroons.

Sieve
To remove any pieces of almond from the processed mixture, a large sieve with medium–fine holes is essential. Sifting the mixture also helps to remove any lumps that may have formed during processing.

Electric whisk
A hand-held electric whisk makes light work of whisking egg whites and making meringue. Choose one with at least three speed settings.

Spatula
Folding the ground almonds and icing sugar into the meringue mixture is the most vital stage of macaroon making and for this you will need a firm-handled rubber or silicone spatula with a flexible tip.

Baking sheets
It's worth investing in a couple of solid baking sheets that won't buckle in the oven to ensure neatly shaped macaroons. Line with non-stick baking paper.

Piping bag and nozzle
For piping perfect macaroons onto the baking sheet make sure you have a large-capacity piping bag. Nylon, fabric or sturdy disposable bags can be used. A plastic or metal plain nozzle with a 1-cm/½-inch hole is also needed.

Basic Ingredients

It only takes a few basic ingredients to make simple macaroon shells.

Ground almonds
These give macaroons their slightly chewy texture and nutty flavour. Although they are available to buy ready-ground in the supermarket, they need to be processed to a finer texture before using to give a smooth finish to the baked macaroons.

Icing sugar
The ground almonds are processed with icing sugar to create a super-fine dry mixture that is easy to fold into the meringue.

Egg whites
In common with any kind of baking, eggs should be used at room temperature when making macaroons. If you have time, separate the eggs a few hours before making the macaroons and leave the whites in a bowl covered loosely with kitchen paper. This allows some moisture to evaporate from the whites.

Food colourings
These can be either in paste or liquid form. A small amount of paste will give a good strong colour so add sparingly. If using liquid colouring, whisk it into the meringue a few drops at a time. Adding colouring will create more moisture in the batter so you may find that brightly coloured macaroons will take a few more minutes to cook.

Flavourings
All kinds of flavourings can be used in macaroons, from ground nuts and seeds to citrus rind, spices, coffee and tea. Add dry flavourings, such as spices, to the almond and icing sugar mixture, and liquid or moist flavourings, such as vanilla extract or lemon rind, to the meringue mixture.

Classic Flavours

Vanilla Macaroons

makes 16

75 g/2¾ oz ground almonds
115 g/4 oz icing sugar
2 large egg whites
50 g/1¾ oz caster sugar
½ tsp vanilla extract

filling
55 g/2 oz unsalted butter, softened
½ tsp vanilla extract
115 g/4 oz icing sugar, sifted

Place the ground almonds and icing sugar in a food processor and process for 15 seconds. Sift the mixture into a bowl. Line two baking sheets with baking paper.

Place the egg whites in a large bowl and whisk until holding soft peaks. Gradually whisk in the caster sugar to make a firm, glossy meringue. Whisk in the vanilla extract.

Using a spatula, fold the almond mixture into the meringue one third at a time. When all the dry ingredients are thoroughly incorporated, continue to cut and fold the mixture until it forms a shiny batter with a thick, ribbon-like consistency.

Pour the mixture into a piping bag fitted with a 1-cm/½-inch plain nozzle. Pipe 32 small rounds onto the prepared baking sheets. Tap the baking sheets firmly onto a work surface to remove air bubbles. Leave at room temperature for 30 minutes. Preheat the oven to 160°C/325°F/Gas Mark 3.

Bake in the preheated oven for 10–15 minutes. Cool for 10 minutes, then carefully peel the macaroons off the baking paper. Leave to cool completely.

To make the filling, beat the butter and vanilla extract in a bowl until pale and fluffy. Gradually beat in the icing sugar until smooth and creamy. Use to sandwich pairs of macaroons together.

Chocolate Macaroons

makes 16

75 g/2¾ oz ground almonds
100 g/3½ oz icing sugar
2 tbsp cocoa powder
2 large egg whites
50 g/1¾ oz caster sugar

filling
100 g/3½ oz good-quality plain chocolate, finely chopped
150 ml/5 fl oz double cream

Place the ground almonds, icing sugar and cocoa powder in a food processor and process for 15 seconds. Sift the mixture into a bowl. Line two baking sheets with baking paper.

Place the egg whites in a large bowl and whisk until holding soft peaks. Gradually whisk in the caster sugar to make a firm, glossy meringue.

Using a spatula, fold the almond mixture into the meringue one third at a time. When all the dry ingredients are thoroughly incorporated, continue to cut and fold the mixture until it forms a shiny batter with a thick, ribbon-like consistency.

Pour the mixture into a piping bag fitted with a 1-cm/½-inch plain nozzle. Pipe 32 small rounds onto the prepared baking sheets. Tap the baking sheets firmly onto a work surface to remove air bubbles. Leave at room temperature for 30 minutes. Preheat the oven to 160°C/325°F/Gas Mark 3.

Bake in the preheated oven for 10–15 minutes. Cool for 10 minutes, then carefully peel the macaroons off the baking paper. Leave to cool completely.

To make the filling, place the chocolate in a heatproof bowl. Heat the cream in a saucepan until just boiling, then pour over the chocolate and stir until smooth. Leave to cool for 15–20 minutes, stirring occasionally, until thickened. Use to sandwich pairs of macaroons together.

Rosewater Macaroons

makes 16

75 g/2¾ oz ground almonds
115 g/4 oz icing sugar
2 large egg whites
50 g/1¾ oz caster sugar
½ tsp rosewater
pink food colouring
paste or liquid
1 tbsp small crystallized
rose petals

filling
150 ml/5 fl oz double cream
2 tsp rosewater

Place the ground almonds and icing sugar in a food processor and process for 15 seconds. Sift the mixture into a bowl. Line two baking sheets with baking paper.

Place the egg whites in a large bowl and whisk until holding soft peaks. Gradually whisk in the caster sugar to make a firm, glossy meringue. Whisk in the rosewater and enough food colouring to give a pale pink colour.

Using a spatula, fold the almond mixture into the meringue one third at a time. When all the dry ingredients are thoroughly incorporated, continue to cut and fold the mixture until it forms a shiny batter with a thick, ribbon-like consistency.

Pour the mixture into a piping bag fitted with a 1-cm/½-inch plain nozzle. Pipe 32 small rounds onto the prepared baking sheets. Tap the baking sheets firmly onto a work surface to remove air bubbles. Top half the macaroons with 2–3 crystallized rose petals. Leave at room temperature for 30 minutes. Preheat the oven to 160°C/325°F/Gas Mark 3.

Bake in the preheated oven for 10–15 minutes. Cool for 10 minutes, then carefully peel the macaroons off the baking paper. Leave to cool completely.

To make the filling, whisk the cream and rosewater together until holding soft peaks. Use to sandwich pairs of macaroons together.

Pistachio Macaroons

makes 16

50 g/1¾ oz ground almonds

25 g/1 oz pistachio nuts,
finely ground, plus 2 tbsp
finely chopped to decorate

115 g/4 oz icing sugar

2 large egg whites

50 g/1¾ oz caster sugar

green food colouring
paste or liquid

filling

55 g/2 oz unsalted butter,
softened

green food colouring
paste or liquid

115 g/4 oz icing sugar, sifted

2 tbsp pistachio nuts,
finely chopped

Place the ground almonds, ground pistachio nuts and icing sugar in a food processor and process for 15 seconds. Sift the mixture into a bowl. Line two baking sheets with baking paper.

Place the egg whites in a large bowl and whisk until holding soft peaks. Gradually whisk in the caster sugar to make a firm, glossy meringue. Whisk in enough food colouring to give a pale green colour.

Using a spatula, fold the almond mixture into the meringue one third at a time. When all the dry ingredients are thoroughly incorporated, continue to cut and fold the mixture until it forms a shiny batter with a thick, ribbon-like consistency.

Pour the mixture into a piping bag fitted with a 1-cm/½-inch plain nozzle. Pipe 32 small rounds onto the prepared baking sheets. Tap the baking sheets firmly onto a work surface to remove air bubbles. Sprinkle over the chopped pistachios. Leave at room temperature for 30 minutes. Preheat the oven to 160°C/325°F/Gas Mark 3.

Bake in the preheated oven for 10–15 minutes. Cool for 10 minutes, then carefully peel the macaroons off the baking paper. Leave to cool completely.

To make the filling, beat the butter and a little food colouring in a bowl. Gradually beat in the icing sugar until smooth and creamy. Stir in the pistachio nuts. Use to sandwich pairs of macaroons together.

Coffee Cream Macaroons

makes 16

75 g/2¾ oz ground almonds

1 tsp coffee granules,
finely crushed

115 g/4 oz icing sugar

2 large egg whites

50 g/1¾ oz caster sugar

1 tbsp coffee sugar crystals,
lightly crushed

filling

55 g/2 oz full-fat soft cheese

25 g/1 oz unsalted butter,
softened

2 tsp cold strong black coffee

115 g/4 oz icing sugar, sifted

Place the ground almonds, coffee granules and icing sugar in a food processor and process for 15 seconds. Sift the mixture into a bowl. Line two baking sheets with baking paper.

Place the egg whites in a large bowl and whisk until holding soft peaks. Gradually whisk in the caster sugar to make a firm, glossy meringue.

Using a spatula, fold the almond mixture into the meringue one third at a time. When all the dry ingredients are thoroughly incorporated, continue to cut and fold the mixture until it forms a shiny batter with a thick, ribbon-like consistency.

Pour the mixture into a piping bag fitted with a 1-cm/½-inch plain nozzle. Pipe 32 small rounds onto the prepared baking sheets. Tap the baking sheets firmly onto a work surface to remove air bubbles. Sprinkle over the sugar crystals. Leave at room temperature for 30 minutes. Preheat the oven to 160°C/325°F/Gas Mark 3.

Bake in the preheated oven for 10–15 minutes. Cool for 10 minutes, then carefully peel the macaroons off the baking paper. Leave to cool completely.

To make the filling, place all the ingredients in a bowl and, using an electric whisk, beat until smooth. Use to sandwich pairs of macaroons together.

Lemon Macaroons

makes 16

75 g/2¾ oz ground almonds
115 g/4 oz icing sugar
2 large egg whites
50 g/1¾ oz caster sugar
finely grated rind of ½ lemon
yellow food colouring paste or liquid

filling
115 g/4 oz mascarpone cheese
finely grated rind of ½ lemon
1 tsp lemon juice
4 tbsp lemon curd

Place the ground almonds and icing sugar in a food processor and process for 15 seconds. Sift the mixture into a bowl. Line two baking sheets with baking paper.

Place the egg whites in a large bowl and whisk until holding soft peaks. Gradually whisk in the caster sugar to make a firm, glossy meringue. Whisk in the lemon rind and enough food colouring to give a bright yellow colour.

Using a spatula, fold the almond mixture into the meringue one third at a time. When all the dry ingredients are thoroughly incorporated, continue to cut and fold the mixture until it forms a shiny batter with a thick, ribbon-like consistency.

Pour the mixture into a piping bag fitted with a 1-cm/½-inch plain nozzle. Pipe 32 small rounds onto the prepared baking sheets. Tap the baking sheets firmly onto a work surface to remove air bubbles. Leave at room temperature for 30 minutes. Preheat the oven to 160°C/325°F/Gas Mark 3.

Bake in the preheated oven for 10–15 minutes. Cool for 10 minutes, then carefully peel the macaroons off the baking paper. Leave to cool completely.

To make the filling, beat the mascarpone and lemon rind and juice together until smooth. Spread the lemon curd over half the macaroons and the mascarpone mixture over the other half. Carefully sandwich together in pairs.

Hazelnut Chocolate Macaroons

makes 16

50 g/1¾ oz ground almonds

25 g/1 oz hazelnuts, finely ground, plus 1 tbsp chopped to decorate

115 g/4 oz icing sugar

2 large egg whites

50 g/1¾ oz caster sugar

6 tbsp hazelnut and chocolate spread

Place the ground almonds, ground hazelnuts and icing sugar in a food processor and process for 15 seconds. Sift the mixture into a bowl. Line two baking sheets with baking paper.

Place the egg whites in a large bowl and whisk until holding soft peaks. Gradually whisk in the caster sugar to make a firm, glossy meringue.

Using a spatula, fold the almond mixture into the meringue one third at a time. When all the dry ingredients are thoroughly incorporated, continue to cut and fold the mixture until it forms a shiny batter with a thick, ribbon-like consistency.

Pour the mixture into a piping bag fitted with a 1-cm/½-inch plain nozzle. Pipe 32 small rounds onto the prepared baking sheets. Tap the baking sheets firmly onto a work surface to remove air bubbles. Sprinkle over the chopped hazelnuts. Leave at room temperature for 30 minutes. Preheat the oven to 160°C/325°F/Gas Mark 3.

Bake in the preheated oven for 10–15 minutes. Cool for 10 minutes, then carefully peel the macaroons off the baking paper. Leave to cool completely.

Sandwich pairs of macaroons together with the hazelnut and chocolate spread.

Fancy Flavours

Saffron & Cardamom Macaroons

makes 16

75 g/2¾ oz ground almonds
115 g/4 oz icing sugar
2 large egg whites
¼ tsp saffron strands, crushed,
plus extra strands to decorate
50 g/1¾ oz caster sugar
yellow food colouring
paste or liquid

filling
55 g/2 oz unsalted butter,
softened
seeds from 4 cardamom pods,
finely crushed
115 g/4 oz icing sugar, sifted

Place the ground almonds and icing sugar in a food processor and process for 15 seconds. Sift the mixture into a bowl. Line two baking sheets with baking paper.

Place the egg whites and crushed saffron strands in a large bowl and whisk until holding soft peaks. Gradually whisk in the caster sugar to make a firm, glossy meringue. Whisk in enough food colouring to give a pale yellow colour.

Using a spatula, fold the almond mixture into the meringue one third at a time. When all the dry ingredients are thoroughly incorporated, continue to cut and fold the mixture until it forms a shiny batter with a thick, ribbon-like consistency.

Pour the mixture into a piping bag fitted with a 1-cm/½-inch plain nozzle. Pipe 32 small rounds onto the prepared baking sheets. Tap the baking sheets firmly onto a work surface to remove air bubbles. Sprinkle over the extra saffron strands. Leave at room temperature for 30 minutes. Preheat the oven to 160°C/325°F/Gas Mark 3.

Bake in the preheated oven for 10–15 minutes. Cool for 10 minutes, then carefully peel the macaroons off the baking paper. Leave to cool completely.

To make the filling, beat the butter and cardamom seeds in a bowl until pale and fluffy. Gradually beat in the icing sugar until smooth and creamy. Use to sandwich pairs of macaroons together.

Chocolate Ginger Macaroons

makes 16

75 g/2¾ oz ground almonds
115 g/4 oz icing sugar
1 tsp ground ginger
2 large egg whites
50 g/1¾ oz caster sugar

filling
25 g/1 oz unsalted butter
1 tbsp stem ginger syrup
85 g/3 oz plain chocolate, broken into pieces
4 tbsp double cream
1 piece stem ginger, finely chopped

Place the ground almonds, icing sugar and ground ginger in a food processor and process for 15 seconds. Sift the mixture into a bowl. Line two baking sheets with baking paper.

Place the egg whites in a large bowl and whisk until holding soft peaks. Gradually whisk in the caster sugar to make a firm, glossy meringue.

Using a spatula, fold the almond mixture into the meringue one third at a time. When all the dry ingredients are thoroughly incorporated, continue to cut and fold the mixture until it forms a shiny batter with a thick, ribbon-like consistency.

Pour the mixture into a piping bag fitted with a 1-cm/½-inch plain nozzle. Pipe 32 small rounds onto the prepared baking sheets. Tap the baking sheets firmly onto a work surface to remove air bubbles. Leave at room temperature for 30 minutes. Preheat the oven to 160°C/325°F/Gas Mark 3.

Bake in the preheated oven for 10–15 minutes. Cool for 10 minutes, then carefully peel the macaroons off the baking paper. Leave to cool completely.

To make the filling, melt the butter, ginger syrup and chocolate in a heatproof bowl set over a pan of simmering water. Remove from the heat and stir in the cream and stem ginger. Cool for 20 minutes, stirring occasionally. Use to sandwich pairs of macaroons together.

Peanut Butter & Jam Macaroons

makes 16

50 g/1¾ oz ground almonds

25 g/1 oz natural roasted peanuts, finely ground

115 g/4 oz icing sugar

2 large egg whites

50 g/1¾ oz caster sugar

1 tbsp salted peanuts, finely chopped

filling

4 tbsp peanut butter

2 tbsp seedless raspberry jam

Place the ground almonds, ground roasted peanuts and icing sugar in a food processor and process for 15 seconds. Sift the mixture into a bowl. Line two baking sheets with baking paper.

Place the egg whites in a large bowl and whisk until holding soft peaks. Gradually whisk in the caster sugar to make a firm, glossy meringue.

Using a spatula, fold the almond mixture into the meringue one third at a time. When all the dry ingredients are thoroughly incorporated, continue to cut and fold the mixture until it forms a shiny batter with a thick, ribbon-like consistency.

Pour the mixture into a piping bag fitted with a 1-cm/½-inch plain nozzle. Pipe 32 small rounds onto the prepared baking sheets. Tap the baking sheets firmly onto a work surface to remove air bubbles. Sprinkle over the chopped salted peanuts. Leave at room temperature for 30 minutes. Preheat the oven to 160°C/325°F/Gas Mark 3.

Bake in the preheated oven for 10–15 minutes. Cool for 10 minutes, then carefully peel the macaroons off the baking paper. Leave to cool completely.

Sandwich pairs of macaroons together with the peanut butter and jam.

Green Tea Macaroons

makes 16

75 g/2¾ oz ground almonds
115 g/4 oz icing sugar,
plus extra for dusting
2 tsp green tea leaves
2 large egg whites
50 g/1¾ oz caster sugar
green food colouring
paste or liquid

filling
55 g/2 oz unsalted butter,
softened
juice and finely grated
rind of ½ lemon
115 g/4 oz icing sugar, sifted

Place the ground almonds, icing sugar and green tea in a food processor and process for 15 seconds. Sift the mixture into a bowl. Line two baking sheets with baking paper.

Place the egg whites in a large bowl and whisk until holding soft peaks. Gradually whisk in the caster sugar to make a firm, glossy meringue. Whisk in enough green food colouring to give a pale green colour.

Using a spatula, fold the almond mixture into the meringue one third at a time. When all the dry ingredients are thoroughly incorporated, continue to cut and fold the mixture until it forms a shiny batter with a thick, ribbon-like consistency.

Pour the mixture into a piping bag fitted with a 1-cm/½-inch plain nozzle. Pipe 32 small rounds onto the prepared baking sheets. Tap the baking sheets firmly onto a work surface to remove air bubbles. Leave at room temperature for 30 minutes. Preheat the oven to 160°C/325°F/Gas Mark 3.

Bake in the preheated oven for 10–15 minutes. Cool for 10 minutes, then carefully peel the macaroons off the baking paper. Leave to cool completely.

To make the filling, beat the butter and lemon juice and rind in a bowl until pale and fluffy. Gradually beat in the icing sugar until smooth and creamy. Use to sandwich pairs of macaroons together. Dust with icing sugar.

Sesame & Lime Macaroons

makes 16

50 g/1¾ oz ground almonds

3 tbsp toasted sesame seeds, finely ground, plus 1 tsp extra to decorate

115 g/4 oz icing sugar

2 large egg whites

50 g/1¾ oz caster sugar

filling

115 g/4 oz medium-fat soft cheese

juice and finely grated rind of ½ lime

2 tbsp icing sugar, sifted

green food colouring paste or liquid

Place the ground almonds, ground sesame seeds and icing sugar in a food processor and process for 15 seconds. Sift the mixture into a bowl. Line two baking sheets with baking paper.

Place the egg whites in a large bowl and whisk until holding soft peaks. Gradually whisk in the caster sugar to make a firm, glossy meringue.

Using a spatula, fold the almond mixture into the meringue one third at a time. When all the dry ingredients are thoroughly incorporated, continue to cut and fold the mixture until it forms a shiny batter with a thick, ribbon-like consistency.

Pour the mixture into a piping bag fitted with a 1-cm/½-inch plain nozzle. Pipe 32 small rounds onto the prepared baking sheets. Tap the baking sheets firmly onto a work surface to remove air bubbles. Sprinkle over the sesame seeds. Leave at room temperature for 30 minutes. Preheat the oven to 160°C/325°F/Gas Mark 3.

Bake in the preheated oven for 10–15 minutes. Cool for 10 minutes, then carefully peel the macaroons off the baking paper. Leave to cool completely.

To make the filling, beat the soft cheese, lime juice and rind and icing sugar until smooth. Add enough food colouring to give a pale green colour. Use to sandwich pairs of macaroons together.

Mint Chocolate Macaroons

makes 16

75 g/2¾ oz ground almonds
115 g/4 oz icing sugar
2 large egg whites
50 g/1¾ oz caster sugar
1 tsp peppermint extract
green food colouring paste or liquid
2 tbsp chocolate sprinkles

filling
55 g/2 oz unsalted butter, softened
55 g/2 oz icing sugar
55 g/2 oz milk chocolate, melted and cooled for 15 minutes

Place the ground almonds and icing sugar in a food processor and process for 15 seconds. Sift the mixture into a bowl. Line two baking sheets with baking paper.

Place the egg whites in a large bowl and whisk until holding soft peaks. Gradually whisk in the caster sugar to make a firm, glossy meringue. Whisk in the peppermint extract and enough green food colouring to give a bright green colour.

Using a spatula, fold the almond mixture into the meringue one third at a time. When all the dry ingredients are thoroughly incorporated, continue to cut and fold the mixture until it forms a shiny batter with a thick, ribbon-like consistency.

Pour the mixture into a piping bag fitted with a 1-cm/½-inch plain nozzle. Pipe 32 small rounds onto the prepared baking sheets. Tap the baking sheets firmly onto a work surface to remove air bubbles. Top with the chocolate sprinkles. Leave at room temperature for 30 minutes. Preheat the oven to 160°C/325°F/Gas Mark 3.

Bake in the preheated oven for 10–15 minutes. Cool for 10 minutes, then carefully peel the macaroons off the baking paper. Leave to cool completely.

To make the filling, beat the butter until pale and fluffy. Sift in the icing sugar and beat thoroughly until smooth and creamy, then fold in the melted chocolate. Use to sandwich pairs of macaroons together.

Violet & Lavender Macaroons

makes 16

75 g/2¾ oz ground almonds
115 g/4 oz icing sugar
2 large egg whites
50 g/1¾ oz lavender sugar
violet food colouring
paste or liquid
1 tsp crystallized violets
1 tsp dried lavender

filling
115 g/4 oz soft cheese
2 tbsp lavender sugar

Place the ground almonds and icing sugar in a food processor and process for 15 seconds. Sift the mixture into a bowl. Line two baking sheets with baking paper.

Place the egg whites in a large bowl and whisk until holding soft peaks. Gradually whisk in the lavender sugar to make a firm, glossy meringue. Whisk in enough food colouring to give a pale violet colour.

Using a spatula, fold the almond mixture into the meringue one third at a time. When all the dry ingredients are thoroughly incorporated, continue to cut and fold the mixture until it forms a shiny batter with a thick, ribbon-like consistency.

Pour the mixture into a piping bag fitted with a 1-cm/½-inch plain nozzle. Pipe 32 small rounds onto the prepared baking sheets. Tap the baking sheets firmly onto a work surface to remove air bubbles. Sprinkle over the crystallized violets and dried lavender. Leave at room temperature for 30 minutes. Preheat the oven to 160°C/325°F/Gas Mark 3.

Bake in the preheated oven for 10–15 minutes. Cool for 10 minutes, then carefully peel the macaroons off the baking paper. Leave to cool completely.

To make the filling, beat together the soft cheese and lavender sugar until smooth. Use to sandwich pairs of macaroons together.

Tiramisù Macaroons

makes 16

75 g/2¾ oz ground almonds

1 tsp coffee granules, finely crushed

115 g/4 oz icing sugar

2 large egg whites

50 g/1¾ oz caster sugar

1 tsp cocoa powder

filling

115 g/4 oz mascarpone cheese

1 tbsp marsala or sweet sherry

25 g/1 oz caster sugar

2 tbsp grated milk or plain chocolate

Place the ground almonds, coffee granules and icing sugar in a food processor and process for 15 seconds. Sift the mixture into a bowl. Line two baking sheets with baking paper.

Place the egg whites in a large bowl and whisk until holding soft peaks. Gradually whisk in the caster sugar to make a firm, glossy meringue.

Using a spatula, fold the almond mixture into the meringue one third at a time. When all the dry ingredients are thoroughly incorporated, continue to cut and fold the mixture until it forms a shiny batter with a thick, ribbon-like consistency.

Pour the mixture into a piping bag fitted with a 1-cm/½ -inch plain nozzle. Pipe 32 small rounds onto the prepared baking sheets. Tap the baking sheets firmly onto a work surface to remove air bubbles. Sift the cocoa powder over the macaroons. Leave at room temperature for 30 minutes. Preheat the oven to 160°C/325°F/ Gas Mark 3.

Bake in the preheated oven for 10–15 minutes. Cool for 10 minutes, then carefully peel the macaroons off the baking paper. Leave to cool completely.

To make the filling, beat the mascarpone, marsala and caster sugar together until smooth. Spread the mascarpone mixture over half the macaroons, sprinkle over the grated chocolate and top with the remaining macaroons.

Fruity Flavours

Strawberry Macaroons

makes 16

75 g/2¾ oz ground almonds

115 g/4 oz icing sugar, plus extra for dusting

2 large egg whites

50 g/1¾ oz caster sugar

pink food colouring paste or liquid

filling

55 g/2 oz unsalted butter, softened

½ tsp vanilla extract

115 g/4 oz icing sugar, sifted

4 strawberries, hulled and finely chopped

Place the ground almonds and icing sugar in a food processor and process for 15 seconds. Sift the mixture into a bowl. Line two baking sheets with baking paper.

Place the egg whites in a large bowl and whisk until holding soft peaks. Gradually whisk in the caster sugar to make a firm, glossy meringue. Whisk in enough food colouring to give a bright pink colour.

Using a spatula, fold the almond mixture into the meringue one third at a time. When all the dry ingredients are thoroughly incorporated, continue to cut and fold the mixture until it forms a shiny batter with a thick, ribbon-like consistency.

Pour the mixture into a piping bag fitted with a 1-cm/½-inch plain nozzle. Pipe 32 small rounds onto the prepared baking sheets. Tap the baking sheets firmly onto a work surface to remove air bubbles. Leave at room temperature for 30 minutes. Preheat the oven to 160°C/325°F/Gas Mark 3.

Bake in the preheated oven for 10–15 minutes. Cool for 10 minutes, then carefully peel the macaroons off the baking paper. Leave to cool completely.

To make the filling, beat the butter and vanilla extract in a bowl until pale and fluffy. Gradually beat in the icing sugar until smooth and creamy. Fold in the strawberries. Use to sandwich pairs of macaroons together. Dust with icing sugar.

Tangy Orange Macaroons

makes 16

75 g/2¾ oz ground almonds
115 g/4 oz icing sugar
2 large egg whites
50 g/1¾ oz caster sugar
2 tsp finely grated orange rind
orange food colouring paste or liquid
4 tbsp orange marmalade

Place the ground almonds and icing sugar in a food processor and process for 15 seconds. Sift the mixture into a bowl. Line two baking sheets with baking paper.

Place the egg whites in a large bowl and whisk until holding soft peaks. Gradually whisk in the caster sugar to make a firm, glossy meringue. Whisk in the orange rind and enough food colouring to give a bright orange colour.

Using a spatula, fold the almond mixture into the meringue one third at a time. When all the dry ingredients are thoroughly incorporated, continue to cut and fold the mixture until it forms a shiny batter with a thick, ribbon-like consistency.

Pour the mixture into a piping bag fitted with a 1-cm/½-inch plain nozzle. Pipe 32 small rounds onto the prepared baking sheets. Tap the baking sheets firmly onto a work surface to remove air bubbles. Leave at room temperature for 30 minutes. Preheat the oven to 160°C/325°F/Gas Mark 3.

Bake in the preheated oven for 10–15 minutes. Cool for 10 minutes, then carefully peel the macaroons off the baking paper. Leave to cool completely.

Sandwich pairs of macaroons together with the marmalade.

Spiced Apple Macaroons

makes 16

75 g/2¾ oz ground almonds
115 g/4 oz icing sugar
1 tsp ground cinnamon
2 large egg whites
50 g/1¾ oz caster sugar
½ tsp freshly grated nutmeg

filling
450 g/1 lb cooking apples, peeled, cored and chopped
3 tbsp caster sugar
1 tbsp water

Place the ground almonds, icing sugar and cinnamon in a food processor and process for 15 seconds. Sift the mixture into a bowl. Line two baking sheets with baking paper.

Place the egg whites in a large bowl and whisk until holding soft peaks. Gradually whisk in the caster sugar to make a firm, glossy meringue.

Using a spatula, fold the almond mixture into the meringue one third at a time. When all the dry ingredients are thoroughly incorporated, continue to cut and fold the mixture until it forms a shiny batter with a thick, ribbon-like consistency.

Pour the mixture into a piping bag fitted with a 1-cm/½-inch plain nozzle. Pipe 32 small rounds onto the prepared baking sheets. Tap the baking sheets firmly onto a work surface to remove air bubbles. Sprinkle over the grated nutmeg. Leave at room temperature for 30 minutes. Preheat the oven to 160°C/325°F/Gas Mark 3.

Bake in the preheated oven for 10–15 minutes. Cool for 10 minutes, then carefully peel the macaroons off the baking paper. Leave to cool completely.

To make the filling, place the apples, sugar and water in a small pan. Cover and simmer for 10 minutes, until soft. Mash with a fork to make a purée, then leave to cool. Use to sandwich pairs of macaroons together.

Nutty Banana & Toffee Macaroons

makes 16

50 g/1¾ oz ground almonds

25 g/1 oz pecan nuts, finely ground, plus 1 tbsp chopped to decorate

115 g/4 oz icing sugar

2 large egg whites

50 g/1¾ oz caster sugar

filling

½ small banana, finely chopped

4 tbsp dulce de leche (toffee sauce)

Place the ground almonds, ground pecan nuts and icing sugar in a food processor and process for 15 seconds. Sift the mixture into a bowl. Line two baking sheets with baking paper.

Place the egg whites in a large bowl and whisk until holding soft peaks. Gradually whisk in the caster sugar until you have a firm, glossy meringue.

Using a spatula, fold the almond mixture into the meringue one third at a time. When all the dry ingredients are thoroughly incorporated, continue to cut and fold the mixture until it forms a shiny batter with a thick, ribbon-like consistency.

Pour the mixture into a piping bag fitted with a 1-cm/½-inch plain nozzle. Pipe 32 small rounds onto the prepared baking sheets. Tap the baking sheets firmly onto a work surface to remove air bubbles. Sprinkle over the chopped pecan nuts. Leave at room temperature for 30 minutes. Preheat the oven to 160°C/325°F/Gas Mark 3.

Bake in the preheated oven for 10–15 minutes. Cool for 10 minutes, then carefully peel the macaroons off the baking paper. Leave to cool completely.

To make the filling, mix together the banana and dulce de leche. Use to sandwich pairs of macaroons together.

Mango & Passion Fruit Macaroons

makes 16

75 g/2¾ oz ground almonds
115 g/4 oz icing sugar
2 large egg whites
50 g/1¾ oz caster sugar
½ tsp vanilla extract
yellow food colouring
paste or liquid
1 piece ready-to-eat dried
mango, finely chopped

filling
150 ml/5 fl oz double cream
3 tbsp mango purée
2 tbsp passion fruit pulp

Place the ground almonds and icing sugar in a food processor and process for 15 seconds. Sift the mixture into a bowl. Line two baking sheets with baking paper.

Place the egg whites in a large bowl and whisk until holding soft peaks. Gradually whisk in the caster sugar to make a firm, glossy meringue. Whisk in the vanilla extract and enough food colouring to give a bright yellow colour.

Using a spatula, fold the almond mixture into the meringue one third at a time. When all the dry ingredients are thoroughly incorporated, continue to cut and fold the mixture until it forms a shiny batter with a thick, ribbon-like consistency.

Pour the mixture into a piping bag fitted with a 1-cm/½-inch plain nozzle. Pipe 32 small rounds onto the prepared baking sheets. Tap the baking sheets firmly onto a work surface to remove air bubbles. Top with the dried mango. Leave at room temperature for 30 minutes. Preheat the oven to 160°C/325°F/Gas Mark 3.

Bake in the preheated oven for 10–15 minutes. Cool for 10 minutes, then carefully peel the macaroons off the baking paper. Leave to cool completely.

To make the filling, whip the cream until holding soft peaks, then fold in the mango purée and passion fruit pulp. Use to sandwich pairs of macaroons together.

Blueberry Cheesecake Macaroons

makes 16

75 g/2¾ oz ground almonds
115 g/4 oz icing sugar
2 large egg whites
50 g/1¾ oz caster sugar
½ tsp vanilla extract
blue food colouring
paste or liquid

filling
115 g/4 oz soft cheese
2 tbsp soured cream
1 tbsp icing sugar
85 g/3 oz fresh blueberries,
lightly crushed

Place the ground almonds and icing sugar in a food processor and process for 15 seconds. Sift the mixture into a bowl. Line two baking sheets with baking paper.

Place the egg whites in a large bowl and whisk until holding soft peaks. Gradually whisk in the caster sugar to make a firm, glossy meringue. Whisk in the vanilla extract and enough food colour to give a bright blue colour.

Using a spatula, fold the almond mixture into the meringue one third at a time. When all the dry ingredients are thoroughly incorporated, continue to cut and fold the mixture until it forms a shiny batter with a thick, ribbon-like consistency.

Pour the mixture into a piping bag fitted with a 1-cm/½-inch plain nozzle. Pipe 32 small rounds onto the prepared baking sheets. Tap the baking sheets firmly onto a work surface to remove air bubbles. Leave at room temperature for 30 minutes. Preheat the oven to 160°C/325°F/Gas Mark 3.

Bake in the preheated oven for 10–15 minutes. Cool for 10 minutes, then carefully peel the macaroons off the baking paper. Leave to cool completely.

To make the filling, beat the soft cheese, soured cream and icing sugar together until smooth. Fold in the crushed blueberries. Use to sandwich pairs of macaroons together.

Raspberry Ripple Macaroons

makes 16

75 g/2¾ oz ground almonds
115 g/4 oz icing sugar
2 large egg whites
50 g/1¾ oz caster sugar
pink food colouring
paste or liquid

filling
150 ml/5 fl oz double cream
1 tsp vanilla extract
3 tbsp raspberry jam

Place the ground almonds and icing sugar in a food processor and process for 15 seconds. Sift the mixture into a bowl. Line two baking sheets with baking paper.

Place the egg whites in a large bowl and whisk until holding soft peaks. Gradually whisk in the caster sugar to make a firm, glossy meringue. Whisk in enough food colouring to give a bright pink colour.

Using a spatula, fold the almond mixture into the meringue one third at a time. When all the dry ingredients are thoroughly incorporated, continue to cut and fold the mixture until it forms a shiny batter with a thick, ribbon-like consistency.

Pour the mixture into a piping bag fitted with a 1-cm/½-inch plain nozzle. Pipe 32 small rounds onto the prepared baking sheets. Tap the baking sheets firmly onto a work surface to remove air bubbles. Use the tip of a cocktail stick to swirl a little food colouring through the top of each macaroon. Leave at room temperature for 30 minutes. Preheat the oven to 160°C/325°F/Gas Mark 3.

Bake in the preheated oven for 10–15 minutes. Cool for 10 minutes, then carefully peel the macaroons off the baking paper. Leave to cool completely.

To make the filling, whip the cream and vanilla extract together until holding soft peaks. Sandwich pairs of macaroons together with the vanilla cream and jam.

Coconut & Pineapple Macaroons

makes 16

50 g/1¾ oz ground almonds

25 g/1 oz desiccated coconut, finely ground, plus 2 tbsp toasted to decorate

115 g/4 oz icing sugar

2 large egg whites

50 g/1¾ oz caster sugar

filling

55 g/2 oz unsalted butter

2 tsp pineapple juice

115 g/4 oz icing sugar, sifted

2 canned pineapple rings, drained and finely chopped

Place the ground almonds, ground coconut and icing sugar in a food processor and process for 15 seconds. Sift the mixture into a bowl. Line two baking sheets with baking paper.

Place the egg whites in a large bowl and whisk until holding soft peaks. Gradually whisk in the caster sugar until you have a firm, glossy meringue.

Using a spatula, fold the almond mixture into the meringue one third at a time. When all the dry ingredients are thoroughly incorporated, continue to cut and fold the mixture until it forms a shiny batter with a thick, ribbon-like consistency.

Pour the mixture into a piping bag fitted with a 1-cm/½-inch plain nozzle. Pipe 32 small rounds onto the prepared baking sheets. Tap the baking sheets firmly onto a work surface to remove air bubbles. Sprinkle over the toasted coconut. Leave at room temperature for 30 minutes. Preheat the oven to 160°C/325°F/Gas Mark 3.

Bake in the preheated oven for 10–15 minutes. Cool for 10 minutes, then carefully peel the macaroons off the baking paper. Leave to cool completely.

To make the filling, beat the butter and pineapple juice in a bowl until pale and fluffy. Gradually beat in the icing sugar until smooth and creamy, then fold in the chopped pineapple. Use to sandwich pairs of macaroons together.

Something Special

Sweetheart Macaroons

makes 6

75 g/2¾ oz ground almonds
115 g/4 oz icing sugar
2 large egg whites
50 g/1¾ oz caster sugar
pink food colouring
paste or liquid

filling
115 g/4 oz white chocolate,
finely chopped
300 ml/10 fl oz double cream

Place the ground almonds and icing sugar in a food processor and process for 15 seconds. Sift the mixture into a bowl. Line two baking sheets with baking paper and, using a 7-cm/2¾-inch heart-shaped cutter, mark 12 heart shapes on the underside of the paper.

Place the egg whites in a large bowl and whisk until holding soft peaks. Gradually whisk in the caster sugar to make a firm, glossy meringue. Whisk in enough food colouring to give a pink colour.

Using a spatula, fold the almond mixture into the meringue one third at a time. When all the dry ingredients are thoroughly incorporated, continue to cut and fold the mixture until it forms a shiny batter with a thick, ribbon-like consistency.

Pour the mixture into a piping bag fitted with a 1-cm/½-inch plain nozzle. Pipe heart shapes onto the prepared baking sheets. Tap the baking sheets firmly onto a work surface to remove air bubbles. Leave at room temperature for 30 minutes. Preheat the oven to 160°C/325°F/Gas Mark 3.

Bake in the preheated oven for 15–20 minutes. Cool for 10 minutes, then carefully peel the macaroons off the baking paper. Leave to cool completely.

To make the filling, place the chocolate in a heatproof bowl. Heat half the cream in a saucepan until boiling, then pour over the chocolate and stir until smooth. Leave until cold. Whip the remaining cream until holding soft peaks and fold into the chocolate mixture. Use to sandwich pairs of macaroons together.

66

Summer Berry Macaroons

makes 6

75 g/2¾ oz ground almonds
115 g/4 oz icing sugar
2 large egg whites
50 g/1¾ oz caster sugar
fresh mint sprigs, to decorate

filling

150 ml/5 fl oz double cream
2 tbsp lemon curd
115 g/4 oz small strawberries, hulled and quartered, plus extra whole strawberries to decorate
115 g/4 oz raspberries
2 tbsp icing sugar

Place the ground almonds and icing sugar in a food processor and process for 15 seconds. Sift the mixture into a bowl. Line two baking sheets with baking paper.

Place the egg whites in a large bowl and whisk until holding soft peaks. Gradually whisk in the caster sugar to make a firm, glossy meringue.

Using a spatula, fold the almond mixture into the meringue one third at a time. When all the dry ingredients are thoroughly incorporated, continue to cut and fold the mixture until it forms a shiny batter with a thick, ribbon-like consistency.

Pour the mixture into a piping bag fitted with a 1-cm/½-inch plain nozzle. Pipe 12 large rounds onto the prepared baking sheets. Tap the baking sheets firmly onto a work surface to remove air bubbles. Leave at room temperature for 30 minutes. Preheat the oven to 160°C/325°F/Gas Mark 3.

Bake in the preheated oven for 15–20 minutes. Cool for 10 minutes, then carefully peel the macaroons off the baking paper. Leave to cool completely.

To make the filling, whip the cream until holding soft peaks, then fold in the lemon curd. Top half the macaroon shells with the lemon cream and two thirds of the berries. Purée the remaining berries with the icing sugar. Drizzle the purée over the berries and top with the remaining macaroons. Serve decorated with mint sprigs and whole strawberries.

Mont Blanc Macaroons

makes 6

75 g/2¾ oz ground almonds

100 g/3½ oz icing sugar,
plus extra for dusting

2 tbsp cocoa powder

2 large egg whites

50 g/1¾ oz caster sugar

filling

200 ml/7 fl oz double cream

4 tbsp sweetened
chestnut purée

2 tbsp plain chocolate
shavings

Place the ground almonds, icing sugar and cocoa powder in a food processor and process for 15 seconds. Sift the mixture into a bowl. Line two baking sheets with baking paper.

Place the egg whites in a large bowl and whisk until holding soft peaks. Gradually whisk in the caster sugar to make a firm, glossy meringue.

Using a spatula, fold the almond mixture into the meringue one third at a time. When all the dry ingredients are thoroughly incorporated, continue to cut and fold the mixture until it forms a shiny batter with a thick, ribbon-like consistency.

Pour the mixture into a piping bag fitted with a 1-cm/½-inch plain nozzle. Pipe 12 large rounds onto the prepared baking sheets. Tap the baking sheets firmly onto a work surface to remove air bubbles. Leave at room temperature for 30 minutes. Preheat the oven to 160°C/325°F/Gas Mark 3.

Bake in the preheated oven for 15–20 minutes. Cool for 10 minutes and then carefully peel the macaroons off the baking paper. Leave to cool completely.

To make the filling, whip the cream until holding soft peaks and fold into the chestnut purée. Pipe the chestnut mixture onto half the macaroons. Top with chocolate shavings and the remaining macaroon shells. Serve dusted with icing sugar.

Christmas Macaroons

makes 16

75 g/2¾ oz ground almonds
115 g/4 oz icing sugar
1 tsp ground mixed spice
2 large egg whites
50 g/1¾ oz golden caster sugar
½ tsp freshly grated nutmeg
1 tsp gold dragées

filling
55 g/2 oz unsalted butter, softened
juice and finely grated rind of ½ orange
1 tsp ground mixed spice
115 g/4 oz icing sugar, sifted
25 g/1 oz glacé cherries, finely chopped

Place the ground almonds, icing sugar and mixed spice in a food processor and process for 15 seconds. Sift the mixture into a bowl. Line two baking sheets with baking paper.

Place the egg whites in a large bowl and whisk until holding soft peaks. Gradually whisk in the caster sugar to make a firm, glossy meringue.

Using a spatula, fold the almond mixture into the meringue one third at a time. When all the dry ingredients are thoroughly incorporated, continue to cut and fold the mixture until it forms a shiny batter with a thick, ribbon-like consistency.

Pour the mixture into a piping bag fitted with a 1-cm/½-inch plain nozzle. Pipe 32 small rounds onto the prepared baking sheets. Tap the baking sheets firmly onto a work surface to remove air bubbles. Sprinkle half the macaroons with the grated nutmeg and gold dragées. Leave at room temperature for 30 minutes. Preheat the oven to 160°C/325°F/Gas Mark 3.

Bake in the preheated oven for 10–15 minutes. Cool for 10 minutes, then carefully peel the macaroons off the baking paper. Leave to cool completely.

To make the filling, beat the butter and orange juice and rind in a bowl until fluffy. Gradually beat in the mixed spice and icing sugar until smooth and creamy. Fold in the glacé cherries. Use to sandwich pairs of macaroons together.

Rum Truffle Macaroons

makes 16

75 g/2¾ oz ground almonds

115 g/4 oz icing sugar,
plus extra for dusting

2 large egg whites

50 g/1¾ oz caster sugar

½ tsp vanilla extract

cocoa powder, for dusting

filling

115 g/4 oz plain chocolate,
broken into pieces

25 g/1 oz unsalted butter

75 ml/2½ fl oz double cream

1 tbsp rum

Place the ground almonds and icing sugar in a food processor and process for 15 seconds. Sift the mixture into a bowl. Line two baking sheets with baking paper.

Place the egg whites in a large bowl and whisk until holding soft peaks. Gradually whisk in the caster sugar to make a firm, glossy meringue. Whisk in the vanilla extract.

Using a spatula, fold the almond mixture into the meringue one third at a time. When all the dry ingredients are thoroughly incorporated, continue to cut and fold the mixture until it forms a shiny batter with a thick, ribbon-like consistency.

Pour the mixture into a piping bag fitted with a 1-cm/½-inch plain nozzle. Pipe 32 small rounds onto the prepared baking sheets. Tap the baking sheets firmly onto a work surface to remove air bubbles. Leave at room temperature for 30 minutes. Preheat the oven to 160°C/325°F/Gas Mark 3.

Bake in the preheated oven for 10–15 minutes. Cool for 10 minutes, then carefully peel the macaroons off the baking paper. Leave to cool completely.

To make the filling, melt the chocolate and butter in a heatproof bowl set over a pan of simmering water. Remove from the heat and stir in the cream and rum. Cool for 10 minutes, then chill in the refrigerator for 30–40 minutes, until thick enough to spread. Use to sandwich pairs of macaroons together. Dust one half of each macaroon with icing sugar and the other half with cocoa powder.

Mini Macaroons

makes 30

75 g/2¾ oz ground almonds
115 g/4 oz icing sugar
2 large egg whites
50 g/1¾ oz caster sugar
½ tsp vanilla extract
selection of sugar sprinkles,
to decorate

filling
85g/3 oz unsalted butter,
softened
1 tsp vanilla extract
175 g/6 oz icing sugar, sifted
pink, yellow and green food
colouring pastes or liquids

Place the ground almonds and icing sugar in a food processor and process for 15 seconds. Sift the mixture into a bowl. Line two baking sheets with baking paper.

Place the egg whites in a large bowl and whisk until holding soft peaks. Gradually whisk in the caster sugar to make a firm, glossy meringue. Whisk in the vanilla extract.

Using a spatula, fold the almond mixture into the meringue one third at a time. When all the dry ingredients are thoroughly incorporated, continue to cut and fold the mixture until it forms a shiny batter with a thick, ribbon-like consistency.

Pour the mixture into a piping bag fitted with a 1-cm/½-inch plain nozzle. Pipe 60 tiny rounds onto the prepared baking sheets. Tap the baking sheets firmly onto a work surface to remove air bubbles. Top with the sprinkles. Leave at room temperature for 30 minutes. Preheat the oven to 160°C/325°F/Gas Mark 3.

Bake in the preheated oven for 10–14 minutes. Cool for 10 minutes, then carefully peel the macaroons off the baking paper. Leave to cool completely.

To make the filling, beat the butter and vanilla extract in a bowl until pale and fluffy. Gradually beat in the icing sugar until smooth and creamy. Divide the buttercream into three bowls and colour each with pink, yellow or green food colouring. Use to sandwich pairs of macaroons together.

Chocolate Macaroon Gateau

serves 14

85 g/3 oz plain chocolate, broken into pieces

175 g/6 oz unsalted butter, softened, plus extra for greasing

175 g/6 oz caster sugar

175 g/6 oz self-raising flour

½ tsp baking powder

3 large eggs, beaten

2 tbsp cocoa powder

14 chocolate macaroon shells (see page 16)

white and plain chocolate curls, to decorate

icing and filling

175 g/6 oz plain chocolate, finely chopped

450 ml/16 fl oz double cream

Preheat the oven to 180°C/350°F/Gas Mark 4. Grease two 23-cm/ 9-inch sandwich tins and line the bases with baking paper. Melt the chocolate in a heatproof bowl set over a pan of simmering water. Remove from the heat and cool, stirring occasionally.

Place the butter, sugar, flour, baking powder, eggs and cocoa powder in a large bowl and, using an electric whisk, beat until smooth and creamy. Fold in the melted chocolate.

Spoon the mixture into the prepared tins and level the surfaces. Bake in the preheated oven for 20–25 minutes, or until risen and just firm to the touch. Leave to cool in the tins for 5 minutes, then turn out and leave to cool completely.

For the icing, place the chocolate in a heatproof bowl. Heat 300 ml/ 10 fl oz of the cream in a saucepan until just boiling, then pour over the chocolate and stir until smooth. Leave to cool for 20–30 minutes, stirring occasionally, until thick enough to spread. Whip the remaining cream until holding soft peaks.

Sandwich the cakes together with one third of the chocolate icing and all the whipped cream. Spread the remaining icing over the top and sides of the cake. Gently press the macaroon shells onto the icing around the side of the cake. Decorate the top with chocolate curls.